Matthew,

Writing this book transformed me. The interviews we are my invisible mentors. I hope that you enjoy reading it.

Anil Beckford
YotC alumni
647 238 2913

TALES OF PEOPLE WHO GET IT

REAL PEOPLE, REAL STORIES, REAL WISDOM, REAL SUCCESS

TALES OF PEOPLE WHO GET IT
REAL PEOPLE, REAL STORIES, REAL WISDOM, REAL SUCCESS

Avil M. Beckford

Foreword by Rodger Nevill Harding B.A. L.L.B.

LuLu Enterprises, Inc.
Morrisville, North Carolina

Published and Distributed by
Lulu Enterprises, Inc., 860 Aviation Parkway, Suite 300, Morrisville, NC 27560,
Email: distro@lulu.com

ISBN 978-1-4303-1598-8
Printed in the United States of America

Design and layout by Tamara Pettman
Photo by Super Foto
Hair and Make-up by Jazma Hair Inc.

This book is dedicated to my father Gerald Beckford, who is no longer with us.

I would also like to dedicate this book to my mother Eileen, brother Gerry and my niece and nephew Camile and Andre.

This one is for you!

AUTOBIOGRAPHY IN FIVE SHORT CHAPTERS

Chapter I
I walk down the street.
There is a deep hole in the sidewalk.
I fall in.
I am lost... I am hopeless.
It isn't my fault.
It takes forever to find a way out.

Chapter II
I walk down the same street.
There is a deep hole in the sidewalk.
I pretend I don't see it.
I fall in again.
I can't believe I am in this same place.
But it isn't my fault.
It still takes a long time to get out.

Chapter III
I walk down the same street.
There is a deep hole in the sidewalk.
I see it there.
I still fall in... it's a habit... but,
my eyes are open.
I know where I am.
It is my fault.
I get out immediately.

Chapter IV
I walk down the same street.
There is a deep hole in the sidewalk.
I walk around it.

Chapter V
I walk down another street.

- Portia Nelson

Reprinted with Permission. Copyright 1993 Portia Nelson, from the book
There's A Hole In My Sidewalk, Beyond Words Publishing, Hillsboro, Oregon.

 Acknowledgements

I'd like to say thank you to the following people who helped to make this book possible:

- Anne Grant who suggested that I write a book

- The 34 people who I interviewed who helped to make this book a reality

- Margaret MacLean for editing this book

- Laurie Wilhelm, Lea Chambers and Stephanie MacKendrick who provided meaningful feedback on how to make the book a lot better

- Family and friends who believe in me and can see capabilities in me that I cannot see in myself

- The many authors and trainers who have created wonderful resources for me to develop my "body of knowledge"

- For the many inventors who have developed technology to make the publishing process virtually painless

FOREWORD

In her new book *Tales of People Who Get It*, Avil Beckford explores what it takes to be professionally successful via kaleidoscopic interviews with thirty-four accomplished individuals from Canada, the United States, Sweden, Switzerland, Jamaica and South Africa. The book is for those who want more out of life, who strive to understand how to conquer challenges and how to use innate ability and learned experience to see the way forward to making a lasting and positive professional impact.

True to her inimitable intelligence gathering ability and inspiring people skills, Beckford quickly uncovers ideas, actions and beliefs that build a collection of scintillating and unique success stories. Each interview is different and engages the reader in its own way. The subjects of her work are for the most part ordinary people who are easily accessible as role models – their stories are not about rags-to-riches, nor about fairy tale lifestyles and vast unimaginable wealth, but rather about the determination to work with what is rather than what isn't! The variety, scope and depth of the interviews ensure that *Tales of People Who Get It* has something for everyone.

Reading each story leaves one feeling with a greater awareness of innate competencies, relevance of experience and a distinct challenge to achieve our own full potential...whatever it may be. The message is clear: You can be who you are and reach for your dreams...If your desire is strong enough!

Cleverly providing the reader the opportunity to select areas of interest, Beckford groups her interviews into five themes – Management & Leadership, Transitions & Changes, Innovation, Personal Belief System and Trusting/Getting What You Need. The convenient format permits the casual reader to derive benefit from each chapter. At the end of each section her "Itness Door" assists in making the content relevant to our own circumstances. Certainly this technique allows readers not only to understand the ongoing evolution, and often the struggle that constitutes success, but encourages the resolve to emulate the process should the same challenges arise in their own lives.

Providing valuable analytical insights based on her own experience, Beckford deconstructs the interviews as a whole. She describes an Itness Continuum that illustrates her observation that the interviewees exhibit 13 qualities or what she has coined as a Baker's Dozen "ItnessPoints," Each ItnessPoint is plotted on scale that ranges from non-itness on one side to ultimate enlightenment on the other. The Continuum indicates where some people have more of "it" than others.

The 13 ItnessPoints are then categorized with 12 Avil Beckford Basics, intrinsically Beckford's own life lessons, into three key themes that emerged in the interviews: Focus, Learning and Passion that are distilled into an Itness Funnel.

This is a different approach to achieving success. After reading the book one is left with a sense of what is realistically possible. The bonus is being provided with understandable and practical steps that will make possibility become reality.

XVII

Rodger Nevill Harding B.A. L.L.B.

Business Intelligence & Leadership Consultant

Toronto, January 2007

Corporate Intelligence Awareness, Securing the Competitive Edge,
Released November 2006

WHY I WROTE THIS BOOK AND THE SUBSEQUENT PROCESS

~THE HISTORY

It never occurred to me to write a business book until a colleague planted a seed. Anne Grant, a director at Mediated Solutions, with whom I get together once a year or so, explained that writing books opened up a world of opportunities and possibilities for her. It gave her credibility and she is now perceived as an expert. She asked me what topics I would be interested in writing about. At that time, I had just started publishing *Ambeck Edge*, my monthly newsletter (www. ambeck.com), so I talked about the various elements in *Ambeck Edge* that I really liked. It took me about three years to develop my newsletter because I wanted it to be different from other newsletters. This book is an extension of *Ambeck Edge*.

Meeting with Anne and talking about writing a business book turned out to be a very useful process for me. The book isn't close to the original outline because it took on a life of its own. I didn't have a preconceived notion of what I wanted the book to look like. I was open to possibilities, responsive to the interviews, and paid attention as the stories unfolded, knowing that something wonderful would emerge.

As I evolved as a person, the book evolved.

While writing this book, I experienced alternating waves of enthusiasm, self-doubt, feelings of unworthiness, and fear of rejection, and I asked myself, "Who are you to write a book? You are certainly no expert." So, what gives me the right to write this book? The answer is simple! My multiple roles: seeker, student, and teacher. Seekers search for answers to their questions, good students are open to learning and doing things differently, and a caring teacher demonstrates what she has learned. This gives me the right to write this book.

1

~THE PROCESS

How did I choose whom to interview? I started off by interviewing people who I knew had a good story to tell and asked them to refer others to me. I also contacted people whom I had read about and asked them if they would allow me to interview them. Most of the interviews were conducted over the telephone, though some people requested face-to-face interviews, and others indicated that they wanted to write their interviews because they "think" better on paper. For those who chose to write their interviews, I often went back to them asking them to expand. The results of the interviews are not scientific, but there is richness in the wisdom of the interviewees.

I didn't use all the interviews because I didn't see how they would add "use" value for my readers. One interviewee decided not to be included in the book because my writing style was too analytical.

I gave interviewees great latitude in interpreting and answering the questions, which turned out to be a wise decision. I got information that I wouldn't have gotten otherwise. For instance, the responses to the questions about the formula for success, and books that made a major difference were illuminating, and at times unexpected.

For example, in Stephanie MacKendrick's response to a book that had a major influence on her life, she explained "It's a conversation I had with Rodger Harding, a career coach, not a book that had a profound impact on my life. He said, "You cannot control the outcome of things, you can only manage the process." When I was able to make the distinction between controlling and managing, it was like night and day. I think it made me more effective and less stressed. The distinction was a profound insight for me because it affected everything for me, particularly at work, but also at home. I think that I understood around it, but the light bulb hadn't gone on."

One unexpected consequence of writing this book is that I found myself being changed by the interviews. Writing this book stretched my capacities and made me MORE than I was. One example of how the interviews changed me was when I was on the homestretch to completing this book, I heard George Fraser's words in my head, "If your goal is to write a book, what steps do you have to take to make that goal a reality? Do only one thing at a time because you can only walk down one road at a time, so walk down that road. FOCUS, FOCUS, FOCUS!" I sat down and wrote out all the steps that I needed to take to finish this book in

2

order of priority, and I focused only on one step at a time. The process worked very well.

Working in research for over 13 years has honed my analytical skills, and, over the past five years, I have developed the art of looking at things in a "holistic" way. To deconstruct the interviews to understand what they were saying, it was critical that I listen to my "inner voice," and see with my "inner eyes," to see what was there, but not obvious to the naked eyes. I wanted to understand what the interviews were telling me so that I could glean profound insights and applications, and be able to clearly articulate what I had learned.

To provide meaningful insights, I realized that I had to use my "whole" brain instead of relying solely on my left-brain. To do this, I spent about five minutes doing some of the exercises in Paul and Gail Dennison's *Brain Gym* before I read the interviews. This book provides simple exercises that allow you to access and use your "whole" brain - both your left and right brain. I coupled these exercises with a simple technique I learned to slow down my brain to the alpha state, a state of peace and tranquility where you are relaxed and can see the "unseen," hear the "unheard" and make connections that you otherwise wouldn't have been able to make.

3

When my mind was prepared, I looked at the information from many different dimensions – many different angles. I viewed the interviews both narrowly and broadly.

What did I see when I used this process? What did I hear when I read the interviews? What connections did I make? I noticed that some interviews were simply extensions of others. The interviews cemented my belief that everything is connected - that we are all connected - we are one. Even though most of the interviewees do not know each other, and they come from different backgrounds and have different priorities, and they live in different cities and even different countries, they speak the same "language," – the language of people who "get it." The tones of the interviews are different, yet they are saying the same things.

I am the common denominator, is that why the interviews are connected? I do not know most of the interviewees, but through a series of one to four degrees of separation, I gained access to them. I got access to the people who were meant to be in the book.

 WHY THESE QUESTIONS?

They are all questions whose answers I was seeking. This book is for me, just as much as it is for you.

1. Describe a business challenge that you had and how you resolved it.

2. What lessons did you learn in the process?

3. How do you integrate your personal and professional life?

4. In your opinion, what is the formula for success?

5. Describe a major regret that you've had.

6. What's your favourite quote and why?

7. Which book did you read that made a major difference in your life?

THE STRUCTURE OF THIS BOOK

I interviewed myself to identify my thoughts, feelings and responses to the same questions. My interview is in Appendix D.

This book is organized into three sections – The Background, The Stories, and The Deconstruction.

The Stories, which is the interview section, is the largest section, and is grouped into five parts, each grouped by themes:

1. Management & Leadership

2. Transitions & Changes

3. Innovation

4. Personal Belief Systems

5. Trusting/Getting What You Need

If 20 people grouped the 34 interviews, they would identify different themes from the ones above. There are several interviews that I could have put into groups other than the ones I chose. I decided to group them by the themes of the challenges faced by the interviewees.

I have splattered information gleaned from the deconstruction process throughout the Stories Section. As I read the interviews, certain phrases struck me as being very wise, worth quoting or noting. I pulled them out and labeled them Words of Wisdom, Quotables, Lessons Learned, and Notables.

For each interview, I included the quotes that influenced the interviewees twice, first in a prominent area where they stand out, and again in the actual interview where I also have their explanation for why they like those quotes. If an interviewee had two quotes, one would appear before and the second would appear after the interview.

You can read the groups of interviews in any sequence that you choose.

In the deconstruction section, I attempt to interpret the interviews and highlight the connections that I noticed.

5

MEET THE INTERVIEWEES

It's often been said that we attract people and circumstances into our lives, both good and bad. It's amazing how I attracted these people into my life. I got connected to them through one to four degrees of separation. Even though I do not know some of them personally, I feel like I do know them because I have heard their stories.

I took a course that Jim Rohn offered and I liked his philosophy so I asked if I could interview him. I learned about Chris Widener through his affiliation with Jim Rohn so I decided that he would be a good candidate for my book. I also admired the way that Chris respects and honors his mother. I read about Arunas Chesonis in an Inc. Magazine article and I never imagined that there were companies with values that honor family and put employees first, the way that PAETEC does. What struck me most in the article was an employee was given a week off after working at the company for only two days, to attend a family member's wedding. I immediately sent Arunas an email congratulating him. When I got serious about the book, I emailed him once again asking to interview him.

I read about Andrea Nierenberg and Gail Blanke on the National Association of Female Executive's website. I was unable to attend their conference so I read the information on the keynote addresses. Both women sounded interesting so I contacted them by email and introduced myself. Both responded and were very pleasant. Shortly after, Gail came to Toronto for an event and I was able to meet her, and I developed a relationship with Andrea through email.

I knew Mary Ellen Bates and Amelia Kassel virtually long before I met them personally. I met them through the Association of Independent Information Professionals' (AIIP) listserv. I admired the way they were helpful when someone posed a question; they were very generous and knowledgeable. Another AIIP member suggested that I interview

Stephen Abram so I took her advice. Heather Resnick, I met through the International Women's Writing Guild. I admired her resilience, fighting breast cancer twice. I had to include these women in the book.

Stephanie MacKendrick I also met through an association, the Canadian Women in Communications (CWC). Despite her hectic travel schedule as president of the association, she finds time to paint. I also admire her because she is a woman who helps other women. By way of a strategic alliance, I became a member of The International Alliance for Women (TIAW) through my CWC membership. Volunteering on the marketing committee for TIAW, I met Lea Chambers. I knew Lea virtually for over a year before we finally met. I included her in the book because I like her philosophy on life and work. I admire her courage to walk away from jobs or situations that are not the right fit for her.

I read Maria Nemeth's book, the *Energy of Money* and found it to be very practical. I enjoyed the book so much that I have referred it many times to family and friends. I emailed her and found her to be a very humble person, and thought that she had to be in the book.

I met Anthea Rossouw at a meeting that I attended and I admired her commitment to leading impoverished women in South Africa toward economic self-sufficiency. I also found her to be a very humble person who walked her talk. I heard Samy Chong speak at an event over five years ago. When I think of Samy, humility, grace and inspiration come to mind. Seaton McLean and his wife talked about their wines at a CWC wine-tasting event. My instincts told me to interview him and so I listened. My cousin suggested that I interview Janice Lawrence-Clarke whom she had met, and a friend introduced me to Tonya Lee Williams.

I heard George Fraser speak at an event in Toronto about three years ago. He shared his story and I am always amazed by how people succeed when they've had a less than an ideal childhood. When I was ready to write this book, it seemed natural that he should be included so I emailed him. Suzanne Gibson talked about innovation at a workshop that I attended. While she was speaking, I felt a connection to her. It's weird to explain, but it was almost like we were kindred spirits. After the workshop I approached her and requested her business card. I told her that I wanted to speak to her at a later date.

After I interviewed Suzanne, I told her that I was looking for some rule breakers and contrarians to include in my book. She introduced me by email to Gabriel Draven. Lydia Danner, another rule breaker and

7

contrarian, I already knew. I have never met anyone like Lydia before, and she is also the calmest person that I know. I thought that she'd add texture to the book. Lydia introduced me by email to four people, of which I interviewed three. Claire Hoy was the only one who made it into the book.

Asha McLeod, my hairdresser, is someone who strives for excellence. I am a great observer, and I always watch the way she trains her staff. She goes in on her days off to train them, which is unheard of in the industry. I would show her a complex hairstyle that I saw in a magazine and tell her that that's the hairstyle that I want when I come in next. She would practice on a mannequin until she got it right. Though she is a well-respected industry veteran, continuous learning is a part of her philosophy because she doesn't think that she knows it all. I had to include her in the book.

At a meeting with a university administrator, where I was discussing a course that I was developing, in that getting-to-know-you portion of the meeting, I indicated that I was writing a book. The administrator suggested that Joe Martin would be an ideal interviewee for my book, and also a good person to talk to about how to proceed with the course that I was developing. He also suggested another person in Switzerland whom I should talk to about my course. I contacted Joe who was expecting my call. Later Joe suggested that I interview Purdy Crawford and John Gardner.

I also contacted the lady in Switzerland, and during the discussion about the course, I mentioned that I was writing a book. She recommended that I interview Nanci Govinder because she thought Nanci would have some interesting things to say. When I interviewed Nanci, I agreed, so I asked Nanci to refer other interviewees to me, and that's how I got to interview Simon Grant.

Ann Kirkland I met at a friend's party and I was interested in what she does for a living, exploring the classics, so I later contacted her for the book. She recommended Peter Bouffard and Gloria Lattanzio because she thought they would be great rule breakers.

9

STEPHEN ABRAM

VP, Innovation, SirsiDynix
www.sirsidynix.com

Stephen Abram leads a busy life giving over 100 international keynote talks annually to library and information industry conferences, as well as writing several columns for library and information professional periodicals. Stephen has chaired successful summits on Digital Libraries, Library Futures, and the crisis in school libraries in Canada, and has been very involved in the promotion of the role school libraries play in education. He was listed by Library Journal as one of the top 50 people influencing the future of libraries and librarianship, and has been awarded the Special Library Association's (SLA) John Cotton Dana Award and is a Fellow of the SLA. Stephen is married and resides in Ontario, Canada.

10

MARY ELLEN BATES

Owner, Bates Information Services
www.batesinfo.com

Author of seven books and innumerable articles on Internet research, and a frequent international speaker, Mary Ellen Bates is the owner of Bates Information Services. Former president of the Association of the Independent Information Professionals (AIIP), Mary Ellen was the first recipient of AIIP's Sue Rugge Memorial Award, created to recognize a member who, through mentoring, has significantly helped others establish their businesses. Quoted in publications such as the New York Times, Wall Street Journal, Washington Post, Wired, Business Week, Washington Business Journal, Computerworld, The Australian and Forbes, she was voted Member of the Year for both the Communications Division and the Washington DC Chapter of the Special Libraries Association and received SLA's 2002 Professional Award. She resides in Colorado, United States.

GAIL BLANKE
President & CEO
Lifedesigns, LLC
www.lifedesigns.com

Gail Blanke, renowned executive coach, and presentation skills trainer, is the author of three books. *In My Wildest Dreams* appeared on both the New York Times and Amazon.com's Best Seller's List. The sole guest on the Oprah Winfrey Show in October 1998 she used concepts from her book to empower audience members to live fulfilling lives. She was one of the youngest female senior vice presidents of Avon Products, Inc., where, in addition to her responsibilities as global head of corporate affairs, she motivated and inspired Avon's half million sales representatives to live the lives of their wildest dreams. She launched the widely acclaimed Avon Breast Cancer Awareness Crusade. She resides in New York City, USA with her husband and two daughters.

11

PETER BOUFFARD
Founding Partner,
Impact Workshops Inc.
www.impactworkshops.com

A serial entrepreneur, Peter Bouffard was Founder and President of Epstein Enterprises Inc., 1991 to 1995, Content Alive Inc. 1995 to 2002 and CE Network Inc. 1999 to 2002. A budding artist - watercolour, acrylic and oil - he has a colorful background in accounting, business development, operations, and creative problem-solving. In his present company, Peter is responsible for developing and facilitating a series of professional development workshops supporting innovation and creativity in the corporate marketplace. Peter resides in Ontario, Canada and is a member of the Institute of Chartered Accountants of Ontario, American Society of Training and Development and The Creative Problem Solving Institute.

PRUDENCE BROWN
Director, Financial Institutions
Supervisory Division, Bank of Jamaica
www.boj.org.jm

Over her 33 years at the Bank of Jamaica, Prudence Brown has worked in many roles, and in many departments. She has gotten international exposure by attending courses, seminars, workshops and conferences worldwide. Prudence sits on several boards and committees and is very involved in the community. She keeps physically active by playing netball and golf and has competed locally and internationally for the bank in netball tournaments. She enjoys gardening, cooking, listening to music, singing and watching various sports. Prudence resides in Kingston, Jamaica.

12

OLIVER CAMPBELL
Principal, Oliver Campbell & Co.

An accountant in public practice, Oliver Campbell is exposed to all aspects of accounting, audit and management consulting. He teaches part-time at the Jamaican Institute of Management, Barry University - Andreas School of Business and Florida International University in their Executive MBA programs. Oliver is a Fellow of the Institute of Chartered Accountants of Jamaica and a member of Registered Public Accountant - Jamaica. A tenor, Oliver sings in several choirs. He lives in Kingston, Jamaica with his wife and has three children and one grandchild.

LEA CHAMBERS

Marketing Director, Golder Associates
www.golder.com

Having traveled to several countries, Lea Chambers speaks five languages - Japanese, French, Italian, German and English. With a background in marketing, Lea studied in both Canada and Japan, and was recognized at the Canadian Mutual Funds Industry Awards for Managing Best Overall Print Marketing Campaigns for 2002/2003. She enjoys skiing, scuba diving, hiking, and rock climbing and lives in Alberta, Canada with her husband and stepson. She is a member of Rotary International and The International Alliance for Women. She was recently recognized as one of the "Top 40 Under 40" in Calgary, Alberta, Canada. For this award, each year, Calgary Inc. names 40 individuals under 40 years of age who have made an outstanding contribution to the Calgary community and assisted with raising Calgary's profile.

13

ARUNAS CHESONIS

Chairman & CEO, PAETEC Corp.
www.paetec.com

Within five years of founding PAETEC in May 1998, Arunas Chesonis led the company to achieve the number two ranking in the 2003 Deloitte Fast 500 list of the fastest-growing public and private technology companies in North America. In the spring of 2004, The Blackstone Group awarded Mr. Chesonis and PAETEC with the Phoenix Award, recognizing PAETEC for its outstanding growth. In 2001, he was awarded the Ernst & Young Entrepreneur of the Year Award and The Rochester Chapter of the Society for Financial Service Professionals presented PAETEC with the 2004 Rochester Business Ethics Award. Arunas has skilfully applied concepts he learned from the course "Rules of the Game," which he took at Rochester University. Arunas resides in New York, United States.

SAMY CHONG
Chief Inspirational Officer,
Corporate Philosopher Inc.
www.corporatephilosopher.com

An executive coach and inspirational speaker, Samy Chong coaches senior leaders who have exhausted traditional methods of solving challenges, and helps them to align their passions with their purpose in life. Prior to becoming an executive coach, he opened his first restaurant at the age of 25 and sold it at age 30. At 32 years old, Samy opened a more upscale restaurant. His fine dining restaurant achieved one of the highest sales volume per seat in the industry, and was consistently voted to the Top 100 Best Restaurants in Toronto Life magazine, a well respected Canadian magazine. Once again Samy sold his restaurant to pursue his dream of making a difference in the world, and started Corporate Philosopher Inc. Samy resides in Toronto, Ontario, Canada.

14

PURDY CRAWFORD
Counsel, Osler,
Hoskin & Harcourt, LLP
www.osler.com

A native of Five Islands, Nova Scotia, Purdy Crawford became an Officer of the Order of Canada in 1996. He was inducted into the Business Hall of Fame of Nova Scotia in 1997 and became a Fellow of the Institute of Corporate Directors in 1999. In 2000, he was inducted into the Canadian Business Hall of Fame and named Ivey Business Leader of the Year. In April 2003, he became one of the five 2002 Public Policy Forum Honourees and in October he was named as The Conference Board of Canada's 2003 Honourary Associate. Purdy resides in Ontario, Canada with his wife. They have six children and 15 grandchildren.

LYDIA DANNER
Teacher/Real Estate Agent
www.high-speedlearning.com

Curious contrarian and fringe dweller, Lydia Danner was born in Austria and orphaned at the age of 6. This turned out to be a great gift, because it brought her to Canada. A trained journalist, she successfully toiled as a freelance writer for 30 some years, but she became disillusioned and embarked on a spiritual odyssey that led her to teach a funky little intensive seminar called High Speed Learning. As a response to those seminars, she is currently writing a little book on the importance of being in the Alpha state. Lydia's passion is to teach High Speed Learning all over the world, and of course, to see more of this beautiful planet. She has three children and resides in Toronto, Ontario, Canada.

15

GABRIEL DRAVEN
President, Village Technologies
www.gabrieldraven.com

Gabriel Draven is the former President of the Green Party of Ontario. He spent 10 years in the corporate world before realizing it didn't agree with him and vice versa. He is a partner in Village Technologies, a renewable energy company based in Toronto. In 2001 he was co-awarded his school's highest award for strategy studies. He hasn't held down a job since. He is an advisor to Net Impact, a campus based-organization promoting ethical business practices to MBAs and young professionals. He enjoys receiving phone calls and can be reached by phone at 416.686.7782. Gabriel lives in Ontario, Canada with his two cats, cycles to business meetings when he can and survives on a meat free, vegetarian diet.

GEORGE FRASER
Chairman & CEO, FraserNet Inc.
www.frasernet.com

George Fraser is one of the foremost authorities on networking and building effective relationships. UPSCALE magazine named him one of the "Top 50 power brokers in Black America". Black Enterprise Magazine called him "Black America's #1 Networker" on a cover issue. Over the past decade, the prestigious publication, Vital Speeches of the Day, has selected, reprinted and distributed worldwide, four of Mr. Fraser's speeches - a first for any professional speaker in America. He resides in Ohio, United States with Nora Jean, his wife of over 30 years. They have two sons, Kyle and Scott.

16

JOHN GARDNER
Retired Executive

Now retired, John Gardner held many positions in his 35 years at Sun Life of Canada, the last position being President and Director. Currently he sits on several boards. John enjoys long distance mountain hiking - Alps, Pyrenees, Appalachians - running, listening to music (concerts and opera), reading, carpentry, and gardening. He is fluent in English and Spanish with working competency in French. He and his wife Encarnita have three children and five grandchildren. They reside in Ontario, Canada.

SUZANNE GIBSON

Suzanne Gibson & Associates
www.suzannegibson.com

Awakening the potential of Canadian non-profit organizations for over 16 years, Suzanne Gibson is an inspired, accomplished consultant with expertise in strategic planning, training and facilitation, fund development, communications, and organizational capacity building. She focuses on transformative interventions that bring vision into reality, and evaluation. Suzanne facilitates creative problem solving and team enhancement with staff groups, volunteer groups, organizations and boards of directors at local, provincial, national and international levels. As founding Executive Director of Raising the Roof, Suzanne led a team of committed staff and volunteers in the development of a new charity dedicated to finding long-term solutions to homelessness. She is an instructor in Ryerson University's Fundraising Certificate Program, and author of Ryerson's Fundraising Curricula. She resides in Ontario, Canada with her husband.

17

NANCI GOVINDER

Director, Aura Suriya Sàrl
www.aurasuriya.com

Nanci Govinder's ten-year corporate career in international marketing and general management in the medical device industry took her from her native South Africa to Sweden, Denmark and finally Switzerland. She has worked as a research associate and then as an external lecturer at IMD, Europe's leading business school, in Lausanne. Now, Nanci is a certified professional business coach who specializes in personal mastery. She delivers seminars and workshops to business and hotel schools, companies, and to the public, mainly in Europe. Nanci resides in Lausanne, Switzerland.

SIMON GRANT

Former CEO
Neoventa Medical AB
www.neoventa.se

A proponent of sabbaticals, Simon Grant has taken two one-year sabbaticals so far, and plans to take more. He has switched careers a few times, leaving a successful career to start over in a new one. Having a degree in Electrical and Electronic Engineering with Biomedical and Expert Systems focus, Simon has taken several courses on Leadership, Project Management and Clinical Education, which shows in his varied background in project management, information technology, operations and senior management to name a few. Simon enjoys kite-surfing, diving, playing squash and traveling, having traveled extensively to over 50 countries. He is fluent in English and Swedish and has competency in Mandarin, Danish and Spanish. Originally from New Zealand, he resides in Sweden with his wife.

18

CLAIRE HOY
Journalist

The first Canadian to make it to number one on the New York Times Bestseller's List for non-fiction for *By Way of Deception: A Devastating Insider's Portrait of the Mossad*, Claire Hoy has written nine other books. He has worked in many areas of journalism - print, radio and television. For five years, during the late 1990s and early 2000s he co-hosted CBC Newsworld's Face-Off, and over the years has been a regular commentator to the Ottawa Citizen, Windsor Star, Sudbury Star, and Hamilton Spectator. He enjoys golfing and cheering for the New York Yankees. Claire has five children and resides in Ontario, Canada with his partner Sally.

AMELIA KASSEL
President , MarketingBase
www.marketingbase.com

A recognized author and international speaker, Amelia Kassel conducts seminars for associations and conferences and gives workshops on-site for companies and organizations, on industry, company, competitive and market intelligence research. Amelia taught at the University of California Berkeley Extension for 15 years, was a lecturer at San José State University School of Library and Information Science (1992-1996), and now teaches distance education at San José State University with courses in Online and Advanced Online Searching. Amelia is a recipient of the Association of Independent Information Professionals' Sue Rugge Memorial Award and the Gale Group Writing Award. She authored *The Super Searchers on Wall Street* and has written many articles for Searcher Magazine, and other information industry publications. Amelia resides in California, United States.

19

 ## ANN KIRKLAND
Founder, Classical Pursuits
www.classicalpursuits.com

B orn in Philadelphia, Ann Kirkland studied art history and city planning, gravitating toward health services planning, policy development and administration in the area of geriatrics. She moved to Toronto in 1975 where she continued her work with the elderly in community, hospital and government settings. In 1999, she made a radical change in direction and launched Classical Pursuits, a small enterprise designed to bring together adults to use great works of literature, music and art as the springboard for discussion of the enduring questions of meaning in our lives.

JANICE LAWRENCE-CLARKE
CEO & Creative Director,
JLC Productions
www.jlcpr.com

Trinidad to New York to Trinidad to New York to Atlanta, Janice Lawrence-Clarke has degrees in both fashion and communications technology. Janice has worked in the fashion industry since 1975 as a runway and illustration model prior to completing a first degree in Fashion Buying & Merchandising at New York's Fashion Institute of Technology. She also produced fashion shows and events, and worked as a journalist and fashion expert. Janice helped to develop the Caribbean fashion industry. She now resides in Georgia, United States with her daughter, and is the Creative Director of her own firm.

20

JOE MARTIN
Professor, University of Toronto,
Rotman School of Business

The author of dozens of articles and cases, Joe Martin has given numerous speeches and presentations. Joe started the first Canadian business history course in Canada. He has been on City TV, ROB TV, Global Morning, CBC's "The Current," and articles have been published on his history course in both the National Post and the Toronto Star. He has a passion for history because he finds it instructive. Prior to teaching, he was a Partner at Deloitte & Touche. He resides in Ontario, Canada with his wife. They have four children and seven grandchildren. Joe currently sits on several boards.

STEPHANIE MACKENDRICK
President, Canadian Women
in Communications
www.cwc-afc.com

An accomplished artist and trained journalist, Stephanie MacKendrick has worked in the communications industry for more than 25 years, 10 of those as President of Canadian Women in Communications. Known internationally for her work to promote women's involvement on corporate boards, she is President of the Board of Directors of The International Alliance for Women, a worldwide umbrella organization of women's networks, and Chair of its Women on Boards initiative. A passionate advocate for diversity, Stephanie received the Innoversity Angel Award for commitment to diversity in September 2005. In November 2005, the Women's Executive Network named Stephanie one of the 100 Most Powerful Women in Canada. Stephanie is married and has two sons. She resides in Ontario, Canada.

21

SEATON MCLEAN
TV Producer/Filmmaker/
Winemaker
www.clossonchase.com

Born in Florida and raised in Montreal, Seaton McLean is one of the founders of Atlantis Films Limited and a partner in Alliance Atlantis Communications. Seaton spent 26 years producing feature films and television productions. His TV and film credits include, the 1980s version of The Twilight Zone, Foolproof, The 51st State and Owning Mahowny. Now, Seaton has switched to making wine, and sees parallels between TV production and winemaking – they are both high-risk endeavours. He and his business partners own Closson Chase Winery. Seaton and his wife have one daughter and reside in Ontario, Canada.

ASHA MCLEOD

Owner, Senior Hair Stylist,
Jazma Hair Salon
www.jazma.com

Doing hair has always been in Asha McLeod's blood. From the age of two, she was exposed to her mother's hair salon in Trinidad. An award winning, internationally acclaimed hairstylist, Asha's work has been featured in Vogue, Essence, Modern Salon, American Salon, Shop Talk and many popular Black hairstyle magazines. Hairstylists travel from all over the world to be trained in her proprietary "Wash & Wear" Relaxer Hair Care System. Her clients travel great distances to get serviced in her upscale salon in downtown Toronto. To remain a cut above the rest, she continuously learns, and continuously trains her team. In her effort to "professionalize" the Black hair care industry, she attends trade shows and does demonstrations. Asha resides in Toronto with her husband.

22

MARIA NEMETH

Founder & Executive Director,
Academy for Coaching Excellence
www.academyforcoachingexcellence.com

A Licensed Clinical Psychologist and Master Certified Coach, Dr. Maria Nemeth is an internationally recognized speaker, author, and seminar leader. Her book, *The Energy of Money*, published in 1999 is available in five languages and won the 1999 Audie Award for best Personal Development Series. For more than 20 years, Dr. Nemeth has trained professional coaches, ministers, clinicians, executives, teachers and private individuals using the coaching methods and skills that she has designed. She is a former Associate Professor, Clinical Psychology, California State University Dominguez Hills and an Associate Clinical Professor, Department of Psychiatry, California State University, Davis School of Medicine. Her work emphasizes clear communication and empowers people to take authentic action to produce extraordinary outcomes.

ANDREA NIERENBERG
President, The Nierenberg Group
www.selfmarketing.com

T he Wall Street Journal describes Andrea
Nierenberg as a "networking success
story." She speaks around the globe at
conferences and for companies, including:
The Israeli Direct Marketing Center, London
Direct Marketing Fair, Pan Pacific (Australia),
Swedish Postal Service, Swiss Bank, and Worldexco (Philippines). As
a respected author and quoted expert, she writes a weekly column for
Fortune Small Business On-Line and has been featured in publications
such as USA Today, The Wall Street Journal, Selling Power, Sales and
Marketing Management, Investor's Business Daily, Inc. Magazine,
The Chicago Tribune, Entrepreneur, Training & Development, Smart
Money and The New York Times. In February 2003, Office Depot and
the National Association of Female Executives honored her as Business
Woman of the Year. Andrea resides in New York City, United States.

23

 HEATHER RESNICK
Owner, HRighter Rights the
Wrong and Writes the Right
www.womenreworked.com

A two-time breast cancer warrior and a
long-time homemaker desiring to re-enter
the workplace, Heather Resnick authored
the book *Women Reworked Empowering
Women in Employment Transition.* Currently
she advises women of the help available and
provides connections for them to other people who can assist them in
achieving their goals. Her vision is for women to follow their dreams
or their life purpose. Life-long learning is her passion. Heather is a
woman always reworking. She is taking guitar lessons for the first
time. Her dream of being a writer where the impact of her words will
positively effect changes for the readers is in full play! Heather resides
in Ontario, Canada.

JIM ROHN
Business Philosopher,
Jim Rohn International
www.jimrohn.com

Having established his fortune and reputation as the head of several business enterprises, Jim Rohn now concentrates his creative skills on Jim Rohn International, a diversified corporation engaged in the worldwide marketing of personal development, management, and sales-oriented seminars and training programs. For more than 39 years, Jim Rohn has focused on the fundamentals of human behavior that most affect personal and business performance. He has conducted his seminars and workshops throughout Europe, Asia, Australia and Africa, as well as in most principal cities in North America. Jim is a member of the National Speakers Association and is a recipient of its coveted CPAE (Council of Peers Award for Excellence) Award, given to him in 1985 for outstanding performance and professionalism in speaking. Jim resides in the United States.

24

ANTHEA ROSSOUW
Founder, Dreamcatcher
www.dreamcatcher.co.za

Anthea Rossouw has harnessed her knowledge of tourism development and understanding of the barriers, which prevent the historically disadvantaged to become gainfully involved in tourism to liberate various communities from poverty and unemployment. She is the recipient of the prestigious Millennium Award, South African Woman for Women, bestowed upon her in Toronto, Canada. She has developed unique micro business opportunities at grassroots level for impoverished and disadvantaged women, which is empowering them to empower themselves and their children. She is also the author of various tourism training - and information publications. A documentary of her remarkable work at local community level, called "Brave New World," by Spliced Knees, was screened on national television on various occasions. Anthea resides in South Africa with her husband.

CHRIS WIDENER

President, Made For Success
www.madeforsuccess.com

Chris Widener is the author of over 350 articles and 7 books, including his newest books, *The Image*, *The Angel Inside* and *Twelve Pillars*, co-authored with Jim Rohn. He has produced close to 20 audio programs on the subjects of leadership and motivation. His articles appear monthly in nearly 100 publications. Chris' newsletter, The Chris Widener Ezine, has subscribers in 105 countries, making it one of the world's most widely distributed newsletters on success and leadership. He is also a featured contributing editor to the Jim Rohn One-Year Success Program. He has been speaking professionally since 1988 and has shared the stage with US Presidential candidates, nationally known television news anchors, best-selling authors and professional athletes.

25

DONALD WILLIAMS

Vice President,
Credit Risk Management,
Bank of Nova Scotia Jamaica Ltd
www.jamaica.scotiabank.com

After a 42 year career at Bank of Nova Scotia Jamaica Ltd. in credit risk management (corporate & retail) and money market fund management, and an international assignment with Scotiabank Canada (parent bank) in the areas of Corporate & International banking, Donald Williams has recently retired. Donald is married and resides in Jamaica. He enjoys playing lawn tennis, reading, as well as spending time with family.

TONYA LEE WILLIAMS
President, ReelWorld
www.reelworld.ca

Best known for her starring role as "Dr. Olivia Winters" on *The Young and the Restless*, Tonya Lee Williams was nominated for the Outstanding Supporting Actress Daytime Emmy in 1996 and 2000. Tonya won the NAACP Image Awards in 2000 and 2004 in the category of Outstanding Lead Actress in a Daytime Drama. She also earned the prestigious Harry Jerome Award in 2004 and the ACTRA Award of Excellence in 2005. In October 1999, Tonya founded ReelWorld Film Festival to create opportunities for Canadian artists from racially and culturally diverse backgrounds. She uses her voice to help change broadcast agreements and government funding policies. Her advocacy work in the entertainment industry has been recognized by an appointment to the newly formed Toronto Film Board. Tonya resides in California, United States.

26

SECTION 2
PART 1: MANAGEMENT AND LEADERSHIP

SAMY CHONG

JOHN GARDNER

SIMON GRANT

GLORIA LATTANZIO

STEPHANIE MACKENDRICK

ASHA MCLEOD

TONYA LEE WILLIAMS

27

SAMY CHONG
Employees, Your Most Valuable Asset

"We can't solve problems by using the same kind of thinking we used when we created them."
-Albert Einstein

~CHALLENGE~ In 1991 when the economy went into a tailspin and the interest rates went into double digits, I owned a restaurant and I remember feeling a sense of hopelessness, a sense of not knowing where the future of the business was going.

~RESOLUTION~ I overcame this feeling of hopelessness by realizing that all the time that I had been investing in creating a place that was really nurturing for my team paid off in spades. I remember a dishwasher who was making $7 or $8 an hour came up to me and told me that if I didn't have the money to pay him for the next couple of months, it would be okay. The faith and trust of my staff, which I had cared for in the past, pulled me through this very difficult time and ensured the protection of the restaurant.

We treated our staff special. When the head chef was getting married, we proposed to close the restaurant to accommodate those workers who wanted to attend the wedding. This was unheard of to close a restaurant on a Saturday night, the busiest night in the industry. When a worker needed a shift covered and couldn't find a replacement, I would step in and cover the shift. Or if a worker was facing a very traumatic time, whether it was a father in a hospital or if a parent died, we would drive them to wherever they needed to be.

Because of my nurturing and caring, the turnover at my restaurant was less than six percent in an industry that averages over 250 percent.

~LESSONS LEARNED~

1. If you nurture and care for your staff, it will pay off in spades

2. I realized that there are no accidents in life, everything about where we are, what we accomplish, who we attract, is all because of who we are, and this is what I call consciousness journey

3. It's truly about how we continue to evolve, to grow, to learn, to make sure that what we do is in alignment with our purpose on this earth, and hopefully that purpose is in alignment with our passion. And if you have the purpose and passion, you basically have a vocation that truly serves humanity

~HOW TO INTEGRATE YOUR PERSONAL AND PROFESSIONAL LIFE~ When you love what you do, and do what you love, it becomes seamless. If I am thinking about an idea, it's about work. My work and personal life is pretty much seamless and not separated. There are times when I do not see clients. I have "Samy Days" where I do not service any clients. I make sure that I take care of myself, whether it be a spa day, massages or going away for the weekend or for holidays. I make sure that I schedule these things so that I have balance because I love what I do so much.

~FORMULA FOR SUCCESS~ For me, looking back at my life, and how I succeeded in different careers and moved forward, the formula for success has two components. The first is having a vision of where I want to go in life. For example, when I was 14 years old and washing dishes, I had a dream of owning a restaurant and never thought that at the age of 25 I would have that dream. And, when I sold that restaurant and bought a very expensive investment property, I had another dream to own a more formal and upscale restaurant. In less than two and a half years, that dream came true.

The second component of the formula for success is when you have your vision, you have to have absolute faith and trust that the universe will deliver. Know that everything happens for a reason. Once you signal to the universe where you are going, you just need to let go and allow things to unfold. And the journey that I've been on is exactly that, leaving a career where I was doing quite well and moving into another where I had no idea how I was going to do, but knowing that I would be serving the world and serving the greater need of the universe.

So, the formula for success is about having a vision, having a dream, having a hope that never flickers out of what you want to achieve. Stephen Covey says this by stating that you should start with the end in mind. I believe that if you have a compelling vision of where you are, where you are going and what that entails, you have won half the battle of what you want to get out of this life and you are on the road to success.

If I were to describe the formula for success as a diagram, I would use three overlapping circles. The first circle would represent what the world needs. Circle two would represent your greatest gifts, passion and purpose, and circle three would represent where the money is. Where the circles overlap in the middle is truly what you came here on earth to do – honouring your purpose, honouring what the world needs and following where the money or energy is. Joseph Campbell says it very well, "Follow your bliss," and there is no doubt in my mind that you will achieve the kind of success that is unheard of.

29

~MAJOR REGRET~ My religion is to live and die without any regret. I have zero regret. I live my life the way I imagine it would be if I knew it was my last day. This is how I live and continue to live the life that I love.

Would there be things that I would do differently if I had to do it over? Because there are no accidents, and everything happens for a reason - what I've attracted, what I need to learn - I look back at my life and at everything that happened, there was always a reason behind it. I do not live a regretful life, I just know that whatever happens was meant to happen. It is for my higher good, it is for me to move forward to the next chapter of my life.

30

~FAVOURITE QUOTE~ I have two favourite quotes that are interrelated. Popularly attributed to Albert Einstein and Benjamin Franklin, I like "Insanity is doing the same thing over and over but expecting to get a different result" and "We can't solve problems by using the same kind of thinking we used when we created them" by Albert Einstein because inside each of us we have the ability to create whatever thought or whatever life we want to create. If we can think it, we can manifest it. With challenges, are we willing to learn, to grow, to stretch to get to where we want to go?

~INFLUENTIAL BOOK~ My bible at this chapter of my life is *Power vs. Force* by Dr. David Hawkins. I like this book because it maps out the skill of consciousness journey of where each of us are, and directs us to what the next step will lead us to. The book calibrates how we continue to live and grow as a human being. It's the most powerful book that I have ever come across in my life.

The Celestine Prophecy by James Redfield also impacted me because it started me on this journey and allowed me to really open my eyes to what this journey on earth is really about.

> *"Insanity is doing the same thing over and over but*
> *expecting to get a different result."*
> Popularly attributed to Albert Einstein & Benjamin Franklin

JOHN GARDNER
The Art of Moving Up Within An Organization

"Bring me a good one-armed economist. I'm fed up with being told that on one hand…, but that on the other …"
-Harry Truman

~CHALLENGE~ One of my biggest challenges was moving within an organization to a position where the responsibilities were completely different from and often at odds with those of the previous position. One day I was responsible for designing and pricing the product. The next day I was responsible for an 800-person retail agency force - that sold the product - located in 40 offices spread across the United States. Sales and marketing had not been an important ingredient in my background, and the question at the time was, "what do I do, especially when most of the people reporting to me believed they should have had the job I had been given?"

~RESOLUTION~ I dealt with this challenge by listening and sorting out the ideas that made sense. I strove to bring the management group together as a team. My background enabled me to contribute to the overall sales and marketing processes, and I was able to put forth directions and ideas that had not previously been in place. Gradually over time things came together.

31

~LESSONS LEARNED~

1. **Adaptability:** I had to be adaptable because the objectives and guidelines for the old and new jobs were very different. I had to identify the new guidelines and objectives and relate to them. You cannot carry the requirements of a prior position into a new one without first assessing the new situation and its needs. You can bring some things with you if they fit the new framework; the rest you must toss aside

2. **Co-ordination:** I recognized the importance of working with management below and management above because a manager does not accomplish much working on his own. The challenge was to figure out how best to deploy those management resources

~HOW TO INTEGRATE YOUR PERSONAL AND PROFESSIONAL LIFE~ I was lucky

to work for a company that had a tradition and a history. Because it had attracted and retained many people with whom I was compatible, I found it easy to blur the lines between personal and professional relationships. Many of the people with whom I worked, and their spouses, became friends.

Secondly, the business I was in, as a manager, was not about numbers or science; it was about people. It was easy to blend the personal with the professional side of life.

I learned early on that my wife could provide insights into people without her having acquired any particular in-depth knowledge of the business. She understands people and can put her finger on their motives. While we did not spend a lot of time talking about business, I appreciated her presence when needed.

Another factor that made integration of my personal and professional life easy was an early decision by the two of us in our marriage that we each had our own sets of skills. We divided up responsibilities and we respected that division; as a couple we got a lot of things done.

My comments should not be interpreted as suggesting my life was mainly professional with little outside involvement. I was continuously active in a wide variety of community affairs. My wife and children all enjoy interesting, challenging lives, and I always made a point of being present. One assesses priorities and strikes the balance that one wants.

~FORMULA FOR SUCCESS~ I do not have a formula for success. There is no

magic route. Common sense is the best guidepost you will encounter. Looking at the factors that contributed to my career path, one has to be prepared to learn all the time, to learn from experiences, and to learn from outside sources. One must be prepared to commit energy and time. One must be rigorous in one's thinking. One cannot be erratic, nor can one rely entirely on intuition. Look to see what is before you, assess it, and make a decision.

~MAJOR REGRET~ My career has been good to me, but there have been

opportunities to move outside the company. I have asked myself what would have happened if I had worked for one firm for 10 to 15 years and then moved on to another and experienced a different environment. I am happy to have worked for one company as I was presented with constantly changing challenges.

32

As a manager it is extremely important to work hard at uncovering the facts involved in whatever the problem or situation he faces, and based on those facts, to make the appropriate decision. One must draw a balance, however, between fact-finding and decision-making. It is not healthy to base decisions on incomplete facts. It is also not healthy to spend too long uncovering facts, thereby avoiding making a decision. If I have a regret, it would be with respect to striking a better balance between the two. I likely spent too much time gathering facts, and may not have made decisions fast enough.

~FAVOURITE QUOTE~ I do not have a favorite quote. Instead, I often think of a story told of President Harry Truman. He was frustrated by the advice he received from his council of economic advisors. Invariably they related to him all the possibilities. In exasperation Truman demanded, "Bring me a good one-armed economist. I'm fed up with being told that on one hand … but that on the other …" Truman wanted to put an end to the fact-finding and get on with decision-making. I can relate to Truman's frustration.

~INFLUENTIAL BOOK~ I would not narrow my list down to one book. I have a wall full of books, the majority of which I have read, but some of which I am still getting to. History is the broad area that I find both fascinating and instructive. If I had to choose one book, it would be *South From Granada* by Gerald Brenan. It has nothing at all to do with business. It is not so much what is in the book, but why I remember it. I met my wife in the south of Spain, a country and culture I knew little about at the time. We did not share a common language, but *South from Granada* dealt with life in a region near where she lived and reading it gave me important insights. The author was a veteran who was partially injured in World War I. Disillusioned with life in England, he left to live in Spain. He spent the rest of his life in that country, becoming an acknowledged expert in its contemporary history. That book kept me going, encouraging me to learn Spanish and go back to Spain. Eventually my wife and I were married. Forty years later we are still married, live here in Canada, and have three children and five grandchildren.

33

SIMON GRANT
PEOPLE AS INDIVIDUALS

"Success is not a place at which one arrives but rather the spirit with which one undertakes and continues the journey."
-Alex Noble

~**CHALLENGE**~ I firmly believe that business is about people. Understanding people as individuals, and providing an environment that they are motivated by, is one of the main business challenges for any leader.

I remember very clearly starting my first job as a recent immigrant to Sweden. I had decided to change something within Research & Development and went in and instructed the appropriate employee – well his reaction was a flat "No" – he couldn't explain why but he just didn't feel it was the right approach. He repeated that "No," he would not follow my instruction. I remember leaving the room with "my tail between my legs" and thinking "but I am the boss, he has to do what I say! …"

~**RESOLUTION**~ Well over time I adjusted to the Swedish consensus management style and actually became very comfortable with it – it is a good way to share risk as a leader and to unite a team. My next stop with the company however was mainland China. One of my first decisions as head of the Beijing office was to re-arrange the office – three of the sales representatives would now be sitting together in a new room. I went in and using my Swedish consensus approach informed them that they should together discuss and decide how they would arrange the desks because it is their room and of course they should decide how it was best arranged, but decide it as soon as possible, as we need to get started. One day went by and two desks were still stacked on top of each other – all three were sharing the same desk. "Come on you have to decide this" I said, "yes, yes," they replied, "We are working on it" looking very worried. Next day the same thing and I was starting to get irritated. Third day still nothing had happened and I lost it – I started shouting out orders. "That goes there, you sit there…" and so on. The look of pure relief on their faces was amazing. They had been totally paralyzed by this seemingly trivial responsibility.

34

~LESSONS LEARNED~

1. Cultures are different and there are no cookbook solutions for working together in groups

2. Even more importantly, people are individually very different and to be a good leader you must spend time observing and talking to those you work with. You do not have to talk about their social interests or their family (though that can help) and become their "pal," but you do need to talk to them about their interests when it comes to their work – and figure out why they think they are/can be important for the company

3. Without your colleagues you are nothing and trying to truly understand them as individuals is the most respectful thing you can do as a leader. Mutual respect provides the foundation for motivation in almost all cases

~HOW TO INTEGRATE YOUR PERSONAL AND PROFESSIONAL LIFE~ With difficulty! I find that the best way for me is to allocate certain days for prioritising family and certain days for work. I tend to do best when I am focussed wholly on one thing at a time. I also prioritise holidays, and have taken two one-year travelling "sabbaticals" so far in my life – and I intend to take more. I have twice left a very successful career and started again from scratch. This can be a very important exercise for the soul and to figure out what really is important (hint – it's not money…)

~FORMULA FOR SUCCESS~ Passion

~MAJOR REGRET~ I don't generally do regrets. One could be being in too much of a hurry, and not spending more time in university learning about "interesting" things rather than engineering.

~FAVOURITE QUOTE~ I like "Success is not a place at which one arrives but rather the spirit with which one undertakes and continues the journey" by Alex Noble because if you focus only on the goals, you will make your bosses happy, but you sell yourself short – life, love and work are all a series of journeys. Goals happen, are temporary and then are gone and leave emptiness. Enjoying life is not about enjoying and having passion for the achievement of goals, but about enjoying and having passion for the journey itself.

~INFLUENTIAL BOOK~ *The Penguin History of the World* by J.M. Roberts was an enormous book for me in all senses of the word. I read it over many months while backpacking around the world. It is over 1,000 pages of fine text, heavy on facts and detail. It describes the development of civilization and the human race and covers an enormous breadth of material and most of the major events in history.

This book helped me put many things in perspective – how temporary things really are and how much has gone before. We tend to believe that our time is special but there is a cyclic nature to power of nations and ideas and even trends. Much of what we see in the world today has happened many times before but with different players and environments. We are not as special as we think.

GLORIA LATTANZIO
THE BUSINESS OF POLITICS

"I believe it, and so I see it." -Marshall McLuhan

~CHALLENGE~ The challenge for me was leaving a very high profile political project. It was clear to me from the beginning that not everyone was supportive of the approach that I was taking. Three quarters of the way into the project, people that were not supportive started to sabotage everything. Toward the end, we had a major fiasco on our hands. The political masters wanted one thing and the people underneath were sabotaging it.

At that point, I had to make sure that the client got what was needed and able to save face. The client's integrity and credibility needed to be preserved.

~RESOLUTION~ I had to go back in and renegotiate what was needed to preserve the client's integrity and credibility, and get the project back on track. I tried to bring all the parties together, but it was clear that this party could not go forward with me. So, I had to essentially cut loose the people who were sabotaging the project. This action had a pretty high price to pay because the people who were sabotaging the project were also very politically involved. I also ran the risk of jeopardizing my own credibility. I did what I felt was required to get the client what was needed.

37

~LESSONS LEARNED~

1. I had an instinct from the beginning, and because things were moving so quickly, I didn't take the time to follow through on my instinct. I had the feeling that it wasn't going to work with a couple of the parties. Had I followed my instincts, I would have removed certain people from the project, much earlier

2. You have to trust your instincts, know and have confidence in your decision-making abilities, and be able to make a decision that would not necessarily be popular with everyone

~HOW TO INTEGRATE YOUR PERSONAL AND PROFESSIONAL LIFE~ Your life is composed of many different facets to create one colourful picture. And so, the values that I hold in my professional life are the same values that I hold in my personal life. I move very easily from professional to personal – in and out. Being a free agent, that's very much the case, so I blend the time that I spend with my children. I can do that, then move off and do some work, then come back in. My personal, professional, spiritual, and recreational lives are very integrated into each other. I have friends who keep the many facets of their life very separate. To me that doesn't work. I like to flow from one to the other.

~FORMULA FOR SUCCESS~ First, you really have to do something that you love. You have to find what that passion is that makes your heart sing and then you do it. The other thing is that you really do need to surround yourself with good people, and recognize that you cannot do anything by yourself, so you need to have people around you. And, you need to have people around you who complement what you bring, because your own weaknesses are made irrelevant by other people's strengths. Another important thing is attitude. Recognize that everybody wants to do a good job, and your job is to find out what the talent is that everybody brings to help them become successful, because their success is your success. The formula for success is very much in your attitude toward life.

~MAJOR REGRET~ My biggest regret is not having the kind of wisdom I have now, when I was much younger. I struggled through much of my teenage years into young adulthood feeling quite unfocused. I regret not having either the wisdom, or the mentors in my life that could have helped me to focus some of the imagination, some of the interests and some of the passions. That expression "youth is wasted on the young," well, it's something like that.

~ FAVOURITE QUOTE~ I like "I believe it, and so I see it" by Marshall McLuhan because for me, it's very much a question of how you see the world. To quote Einstein, "the world in my view is a very friendly place," so, it's a place of joy, a place of optimism, a place of imagination and opportunity. That's not to say that there isn't pain, and suffering and bleakness. There are those things, but life is a long journey that we go on, and we need to appreciate and recognize the lessons that we learn on that journey, and be able to see whatever lessons experience teaches us so that we become better, and leave the world a better place than when we came into it. This is what Marshall's quotation does for me.

~INFLUENTIAL BOOK~ When I think about a book that had a profound impact on my life, there are three books that have a similar theme. They are Germaine Greer's *The Female Eunuch*, Gloria Steinem's *Outrageous Acts and Everyday Rebellions* and Marilyn French's *The Women's Room*. These books all dealt with the issue of feminism, and gave me an intellectual framework to understand the role of women in society, and then from there, to begin to socially advocate for an increasing role for women in society.

STEPHANIE MACKENDRICK
INTRODUCING NEW TECHNOLOGY

"Never doubt that a small group of thoughtful, committed citizens can change the world. Indeed, it is the only thing that ever has." -Margaret Meade

~CHALLENGE~ When we were redoing the association's website many years ago, website development wasn't as well established as it is today, and the understanding of the process from a management perspective also wasn't very well understood. We engaged a firm that had experience in developing websites for associations, to create a new one for us. We went through all the things that we wanted them to do, and the week we were supposed to go live with the new website, it wasn't functioning. They called and told us that they couldn't develop our new website because they had over-promised, and now had to withdraw. Almost a year later, we were right back where we started, and not only that, they overwrote our old website, and so, we had to reconstruct it.

39

~RESOLUTION~ I realized that you can hire experts from outside for a project, but to be effective, there has to be enough expertise within your organization to make the outcome what you need. Coming to this realization, we hired someone with the technical knowledge and skills to oversee the process. She did a superb job of making sure that not only did we get the advice from the web developer, but also that we had someone with expertise who made sure that the website was functional, was practical, looked ahead, and provided us with the right tools to meet our needs.

~LESSONS LEARNED~

1. You have to bring in someone internally with specialized credentials to oversee the process for projects that are specialized or need very technical skills. You cannot even oversee it if you do not have a certain level of knowledge

2. This process was very instructive in terms of the difficulty in managing a project even when you bring experts in. You don't know what you don't know with something this new and so specialized

~HOW TO INTEGRATE YOUR PERSONAL AND PROFESSIONAL LIFE~ One of the most important things is to try and be yourself in both situations, that is, not to have a business personality and a real personality, but to have one and the same. There are situations where you certainly have to behave differently and respond in a way that's businesslike, but this doesn't mean that you have to be a different person, and I find this very important. I try to draw a fairly clear line between work and home. If I need to, I take work home, but I try not to, I try to finish my work before I leave. So, if I am working at home in the evenings or on weekends, it's the exception and not the rule. To me, this is important because I need to feel that there is a time when I am off duty.

To me, it is really more about co-existing, where you manage both your personal and professional life. In terms of integration, I am living the dream of working at a job I would want to do anyway even if I weren't getting paid. Being motivated and caring about what I do, and having a personal interest, as well as a professional interest is very ideal.

~FORMULA FOR SUCCESS~ I think that one of the most important things is to understand yourself, not only in terms of your strengths and weaknesses, what you are good at, but also in terms of what you like to do, and finding something that really plays to your interests and your strengths is really important. I know that people get very good at things and there is a demand for it, but may not enjoy doing it. What you're good at and what you enjoy doing are not always the same. I think that if you can align what you enjoy doing, and what you're good at, your chances of success and having really high impact is much better. All of this requires a very strategic outlook on everything that you do.

~MAJOR REGRET~ If there is anything that I regret, it is that I really didn't understand earlier in my career the kinds of situations that would allow me to flourish, and the importance of aligning my interests with my strengths. I think that it made me a very good employee in some situations and a very ineffective employee in others.

~FAVOURITE QUOTE~ I like "Never doubt that a small group of thoughtful, committed citizens can change the world. Indeed, it is the only thing that ever has" by Margaret Meade because it says that change can happen from every one of us, from small groups. It doesn't have to be a big project, a big organization with a big mission or mandate. We can all contribute to changing.

~INFLUENTIAL BOOK~ It's a conversation I had with Rodger Harding, a career coach, not a book that had a profound impact on my life. He said, "You cannot control the outcome of things, you can only manage the process." When I was able to make the distinction between controlling and managing, it was like night and day. I think it made me more effective and less stressed. The distinction was a profound insight for me because it affected everything for me, particularly at work, but also at home. I think that I understood around it, but the light bulb hadn't gone on.

ASHA MCLEOD
HOW TO INTEGRATE YOUR PERSONAL AND PROFESSIONAL LIFE

"Let gratitude be your attitude." -Author Unknown

~CHALLENGE~ Looking back over the years at the various problems and obstacles that come with owning a fast paced, successful hair salon, I have to say the most challenging of them all was dealing with my staff. What I found most challenging was that I was constantly doing all I could do to train them to be the best stylists they could be. This involved countless hours of professional training, personal and emotional support. The end result would always be that I would have trained and developed successful, confident stylists. So successful and confident that they would always believe they were capable of more than working for me, and would leave our salon, usually taking our clientele that they had built up as a result of working with us. It was very hard to deal with this, and it would happen over and over. It left me feeling hurt, and as a result I found I was bitter toward new staff as I viewed them inevitably doing the same thing so many others had done in the past.

~RESOLUTION~ Eventually I realized that I was creating the problem and making it worse by telling myself things that would add to the bitterness and resentment through my negative thinking. I finally realized that staff will leave no matter what I do. I changed my perspective and motivating factors for why I teach them. Instead of teaching them to be successful because it would be better for my business, I now train them believing I am helping them to become better people. I also train them not expecting gratitude in return, and knowing they will move on eventually.

~LESSONS LEARNED~

1. Staff will always leave but that doesn't mean that I shouldn't train them to do their jobs better

2. I now do things without expecting something in return

3. Resentment and negative thinking harms you and prevents you from being the best you can be

~ HOW TO INTEGRATE YOUR PERSONAL AND PROFESSIONAL LIFE ~ I don't really see much difference between my professional and personal life. For me they are closely intertwined. The same passion and persistence that leads me to excel is applied to both the personal and professional areas of my

life. It's more a philosophy, a way of thinking and viewing this world, that makes work more of an extension of living, rather than living as an extension of work. I live my life, and work is an aspect of it. It's not the other way around. I believe I have been blessed with my skills and talent because I have a duty to share them with humanity. I see myself as a key that enables others to unlock their abilities and become better and more beautiful people. To me I find life more fulfilling and work more rewarding by viewing the world and living life this way.

~FORMULA FOR SUCCESS~ Keep in mind that success is never a final destination, but a journey, and as long as you are committed to lifelong learning, and passionate about your work, success is inevitable. I measure my success not against others, but by my own progress in overcoming day-to-day challenges, continuously learning and growing from those experiences. I believe my passion, persistence and need to please my clients have largely been the foundation for the success I have enjoyed in my profession.

~MAJOR REGRET~ My major regret in life is not realizing sooner that life is about how you work, deal and interact with other human beings. Before I figured this out, I treated people I worked with and those on the streets with unkindness and inconsideration. I ended up not liking the person that I was.

Even though I have evolved, it's still a regret knowing that I have hurt people unnecessarily.

I learned that a little bit of honey goes a long way. Had I known this 20 years ago, it would have saved me a lot of heartache.

~FAVOURITE QUOTE~ I like "Let gratitude be your attitude" because I feel that I am a negative person. Even though I have been lucky and blessed with talent, I feel as if I am not as appreciative as I should be. I am always looking at the negative side of life. The quote keeps me grounded and reminds me of all the good in my life.

~INFLUENTIAL BOOK ~ The book, which had a major impact on my life, is *The Seven Habits of Highly Effective People* by Stephen Covey. This book is my bible. Because of my negative view of life, I realize that I can always be better. I strive to make myself better. I had to find habits to make me more successful. It teaches me how to interact with my team at work, and shows me how to be a better team player and motivate my apprentices. They work with me and not for me.

43

TONYA LEE WILLIAMS
HIRING THE RIGHT EMPLOYEE

"The most powerful weapon on earth is the human soul on fire."
-Ferdinand Foch

~CHALLENGE~ Being an only child and working in the entertainment industry has made me hone my talents to take care of all facets of my professional life by myself. I am the quintessential "Lone Wolf." Knowing what qualities to look for in hiring staff members and learning to trust and delegate to my staff has been quite a challenge for me.

~RESOLUTION~ The first step in my finding a solution was to hone my hiring skills. I've learnt over the years to really listen to the candidates I'm considering for jobs. The interviewing process can reap a lot of vital information. Make sure the candidate fully understands the organization, its vision, and make sure the candidate is looking to grow within the company and stay awhile. I learned to be better at clearly defining my needs and getting my candidates to clearly define their needs. And I learned not to be afraid if the needs don't match, I just thank them for coming in and move on to a more suitable candidate. Don't settle, you'll regret it later.

~LESSONS LEARNED~

1. Make sure that the job description I post is clear and precise as to what I'm seeking

2. During the interview process make sure my candidate understands what my requirements are, and make sure that I understand what their expectations are

3. Make the interview process relaxed and conversational…try to get a feel for the individual… will they be a good fit with me and with the other staff

4. Make sure the individual is trained and qualified in the areas I require, so that I will have confidence that they can deliver results, think for themselves and problem solve without my help

5. Make sure my staff knows how much I appreciate them and the work they do. Encourage them to think outside the box. Motivate them with the opportunity to move up through the company

~HOW TO INTEGRATE YOUR PERSONAL AND PROFESSIONAL LIFE~ Since I'm an artist and the work I do is directly related to my personal life, I don't try to divide my work from my personal life. My work is actually an extension of the things I feel passionate about. I love movies, television and all forms of storytelling. Everything I do is in some way related to these areas. Whether it's political, or acting, or running a film festival, directing or producing, I love to integrate what my personal experiences are. I use my work to help me understand the world around me. The personal relationships I have, are also integrated into my professional work. I feel very blessed to be able to have the two work in harmony.

~FORMULA FOR SUCCESS~ Find something you're passionate about. Don't limit yourself by worrying that the thing you're passionate about may not bring you financial rewards. The first step is to find that thing. Then when you've found something you love more than anything else in the world, focus on the many areas you can do this thing and make a living. Also, don't limit the thing you want to do, to a specific city or country. For example, you may love working with your hands. There are so many things you can do with your hands. You could train to be a shoemaker. Shoemaking is a highly respected artisan craft in many areas of the world. You could make one of a kind furniture pieces. If you love poetry, but wonder how you could make a living doing that, you might start a poetry festival in New Brunswick for example. Don't limit your dreams in any way. There's always a way to make money from them. Let your imagination soar!

45

~MAJOR REGRET~ All of life comes with its highs and its lows. It's not possible to have your highs without your lows. So I can't think of any regrets, because for me the lows in my life, enriched and strengthened me to achieve my highs. I love the journey of my life, and wouldn't wish to change a single moment for fear that I may also change and lose the wonderful moments.

But if there were a quality about myself that I would like to work on, it would be that I could be more discerning about the people I allow in my life. It's hard for me to accept that there are just some people on this planet that would rather be victims of life, than embrace the fact that they are the only obstacles holding them from their rewards.

~FAVOURITE QUOTE~ I have many favourite quotes. Right now, my favourite quote is "The most powerful weapon on earth is the human soul on fire" by Ferdinand Foch. Any quote that talks about infusing spirit with passion is a great quote.

~INFLUENTIAL BOOK~ I love books, and I've been a voracious reader since the age of four. I love books that open your heart and your mind. *Love in the Time of Cholera* and *One hundred Years of Solitude*, both by Gabriel Garcia Marquez are wonderful books…, also I love all of Paulo Coelho's books. Books on any kind of spirituality or religion are fascinating to me. The history of Christianity and Judaism is always interesting. *A World Light Only by Fire* by William Manchester is a great book. Kahlil Gibran's *The Prophet* is so powerful. *Autobiography of a Yogi* by Paramhansa Yogananda is incredible. Works by Ghandi, very stimulating. *On Her Knees* is a fantastic Canadian novel. I LOVE mystery novels and I've pretty much read all of Agatha Christie, P. D. James, Ngaio Marsh, Anne Perry, Sue Grafton, just to name a few. I love Margaret Atwood's and Michael Ondaatje's works. I love poetry and have too many favourite poets to list here. I also love the classics, Charles Dickens, Jane Austen, D. H. Lawrence (yes I consider him a classic), are the ones I think of immediately. As a child I loved the Greek writers and books – Homer's *Odyssey*. I was fascinated with mythology and read lots of it.

If I had to choose, it would be *The Big Jump* by Benjamin Elkin, and *The Brothers Karamazov* by Fyodor Dosteovsky

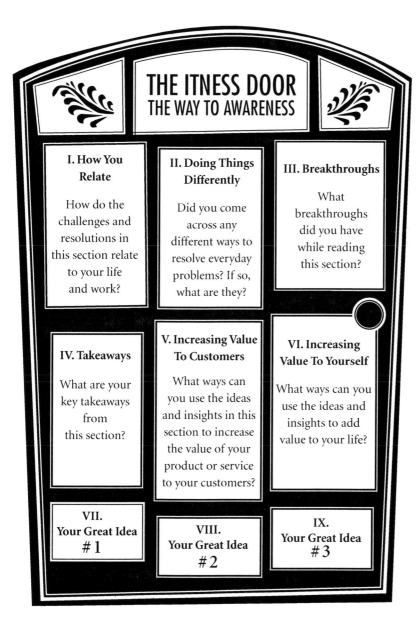

THE ITNESS DOOR
THE WAY TO AWARENESS

I. How You Relate

How do the challenges and resolutions in this section relate to your life and work?

II. Doing Things Differently

Did you come across any different ways to resolve everyday problems? If so, what are they?

III. Breakthroughs

What breakthroughs did you have while reading this section?

IV. Takeaways

What are your key takeaways from this section?

V. Increasing Value To Customers

What ways can you use the ideas and insights in this section to increase the value of your product or service to your customers?

VI. Increasing Value To Yourself

What ways can you use the ideas and insights to add value to your life?

VII. Your Great Idea #1

VIII. Your Great Idea #2

IX. Your Great Idea #3

47

48

49

WORDS OF WISDOM 🌿

Problems are often complex, and you have to find a multifaceted solution. ~Stephen Abram

… Do what you love, be prepared to do things you don't particularly enjoy doing in order to build and sustain your business, surround yourself with the things that revive your soul, don't take yourself too seriously and give back to the profession. ~Mary Ellen Bates

Identify your "catcher," the person who backs you up, and "let the catcher do the catching." ~Gail Blanke

It's easy to focus on what you think is important, but it's always about the other person, and their needs, and this takes you down the right strategic path. ~Peter Bouffard

You need to involve other parties from an early stage, in the decision-making process, in situations in which they are affected, and recognize their views and input. ~Prudence Brown

The loss of a client is not necessarily a negative. New business opportunities constantly arise and the loss of a client may in fact allow you to accept new business. ~Oliver Campbell

… One's attitude about what exactly their "job" is influences how they integrate their work and professional life… Our "JOB" in life is to awaken to who we truly are – to experience the greatest level of freedom and achievement we can in all aspects of our lives and to BE who we are as fully as we can be in each moment. ~Lea Chambers

People work for YOU to pay for other parts of their lives. ~Arunas Chesonis

… There are no accidents in life, everything about where we are, what we accomplish, who we attract, is all because of who we are, and this is what I call consciousness journey. ~Samy Chong

Have a strategy on how you do things [and] execute the strategy with passion. ~Purdy Crawford

50

If you are having a challenge on a business level, do not look at how to change others, or even how to change the situation. Look at a way to change yourself. ~Lydia Danner

If you want to make it happen, just go out and do it. ~Gabriel Draven

Do only one thing at a time because you can only walk down one road at a time, so walk down that road. FOCUS, FOCUS, FOCUS. ~George Fraser

You cannot carry the requirements of a prior position into a new one without first assessing the new situation and its needs. You can bring some things with you if they fit the new framework; the rest you must toss aside. ~John Gardner

As a manager it is extremely important to work hard at uncovering the facts involved in whatever the problem or situation he [or she] faces, and based on those facts, to make the appropriate decision. One must draw a balance, however, between fact-finding and decision-making. ~John Gardner

51

If you are trying to start a business or trying to do something new you're innovating. When you innovate you are in a leadership role. In that role, you have to involve other people and give them ownership, and create what I call "roving" leadership where you let people pick-up things and run with them. ~Suzanne Gibson

Things only ever happen because many hands till the soil. Synergy is at the heart of all successful endeavours. ~Suzanne Gibson

Don't be afraid to show your vulnerability and ask for help. If your intention is clear and honest, people will rally around you and unify toward a common goal. ~Nanci Govinder

Without your colleagues you are nothing and trying to truly understand them as individuals is the most respectful thing you can do as a leader. And mutual respect provides the foundation for motivation in almost all cases. ~Simon Grant

Most people have some skills to offer and just because you made bad investments or had some bad luck, you still have the same skills that got you ahead before. ~Claire Hoy

People who are sitting in their offices at 10:00 p.m. trying to finish a report that is so important, should ask themselves if five years from now if they are going to have any recollection of what was so important about the report. ~Claire Hoy

At a business level, there is always risk, but you can take the risk and follow your intuition. -Amelia Kassel

Knowing who you are and what your gifts are, your limitations, and then finding a way to put that to a use that is a benefit to the world, somehow helps. ~Ann Kirkland

You have to trust your instincts, know and have confidence in your decision-making abilities, and be able to make a decision that would not necessarily be popular with everyone. -Gloria Lattanzio

It is most advantageous to line up the right product or service with the right market. Even though you may think that you have a brilliant idea or program, you need to do research to ensure that your product/ idea is solid for the people to whom you're selling. ~Janice Lawrence-Clarke

What you're good at and what you enjoy doing are not always the same... If you can align what you enjoy doing with what you're good at, your chances of success and having a really high impact is much better. ~Stephanie MacKendrick

You have to bring in someone internally with specialized credentials to oversee the process for projects that are specialized or need very technical skills. You cannot even oversee it if you do not have a certain level of knowledge. ~Stephanie MacKendrick

I always make time for my family, and the trick is to do the unexpected, not just the expected. ~Joe Martin

Stay true to yourself and do not change your beliefs, philosophies or approach just to get ahead. ~Seaton McLean

Resentment and negative thinking harms you and prevents you from being the best you can be. ~Asha McLeod

I do not have to do anything extraordinary. All I need to do is wake up and see what's been here waiting for me all the time. It's already here and all is well. ~Maria Nemeth

You always have to find the silver lining in the clouds.
~Andrea Nierenberg

The only way to survive in business is to be profitable, unless you have an unlimited amount of money. ~Jim Rohn

You attract success because of the person you are. Personal development is the key. -Jim Rohn

For economic safety for the future, you must have multiple skills and languages. Success is basically being the best that you can be.
~Jim Rohn

It will help us little in Africa to try to save the environment, the rhinos and the elephants if people who are custodians, do not benefit from these actions. Hungry, destitute people do not understand the need to preserve the forest if they are hungry, or they look the other way when they are enticed to poach, or become involved in clandestine activities when offered money. It's about survival at grassroots. ~Anthea Rossouw

A woman can make a difference even if she finds herself caged in her poor community. She has herself. No one can take that from her – only herself. ~Anthea Rossouw

Make sure that you do all the due diligence prior to going into [a] partnership. Make sure that you understand the other party's expectations of you and make sure that they understand your expectations of them. The more upfront work that you do, the better off you are after the deal is struck. ~Chris Widener

53

SECTION 2
PART 2: TRANSITIONS & CHANGES

PETER BOUFFARD

PRUDENCE BROWN

PURDY CRAWFORD

NANCI GOVINDER

CLAIRE HOY

AMELIA KASSEL

ANN KIRKLAND

SEATON MCLEAN

JIM ROHN

DONALD WILLIAMS

PETER BOUFFARD
CUSTOMIZING YOUR PRODUCT: A SHIFT IN MINDSET

"Have the courage to live what you believe." -Peter Bouffard

~CHALLENGE~ One of the biggest challenges that I had to face was to make my workshop more applicable, and used by the people who take it.

~RESOLUTION~ I resolved this challenge by focusing on what really mattered and what was important to the people in their world, in their lives at work. So, I designed workshops that fit into their reality.

~LESSONS LEARNED~

1. It's easy to focus on what you think is important, but it's always about the other person, and their needs, and this takes you down the right strategic path

~HOW TO INTEGRATE YOUR PERSONAL AND PROFESSIONAL LIFE~ In the past, my personal and professional life used to be very different, but now, I live what I do. I am doing who I am. I do workshops on creative thinking and problem-solving. I am an artist, I am a businessman, and it's all one now.

~FORMULA FOR SUCCESS~ I am not going to define success. But, I think what's important is to understand what you are really passionate about, what gives you energy, and to listen to that, and find out how you can live it. It's been said a million times before, but it's easy to talk about and hard to do.

~MAJOR REGRET~ My biggest regret is that when I first started out in my career, I focused too much on what I knew instead of who I knew. If I could do it again, I would have developed and spent more time on the right relationships in work, rather than just thinking that I have all the answers.

~FAVOURITE QUOTE~ It would be along lines of having the courage to live what you believe. I am sure there is a quote somewhere that speaks to that. I like it because when one does that, you connect with your energy, you connect with who you are, and everything flows, everything is natural and nothing is forced.

~**INFLUENTIAL BOOK**~ It's a book called *The Way to Love* by Anthony de Mello, a Jesuit priest from India. The reason that I enjoyed this book was, it's in the context of finding love, it's done within an area that makes it real, and he focuses on love at the point of reality, both in yourself and the other person, rather than aspects of pure romantic desire type love, needy love, and all that other kind of stuff that gets romanticized so much. In the book, you see that love is really about what it gives, what it's like given to you and to the other person.

57

PRUDENCE BROWN
EFFECTIVELY MANAGING CHANGE

"Only the best is good enough." -Author Unknown

~CHALLENGE~ When the Bank of Jamaica (BOJ) undertook the supervision and monitoring of credit unions under the umbrella of the financial sector, there was great resistance and hostility from the credit union sub-sector because they felt that they were a co-operative operating under self-regulation and should not be regulated.

~RESOLUTION~ Management took a non-confrontational approach to examine the credit unions. Instead of sending the usual Team Leader assigned to lead the inspection team, Directors were requested to lead the team to ensure that at the opening interview, the credit unions would be apprised of the real reason for the examination, noting that this was the worldwide approach to supervision to bring the financial sector under one regulatory umbrella, ensure that the highest level of professionalism was maintained, and inform the institutions that we were there to assist them to prepare for the licensing process by the Minister of Finance.

~SECONDARY CHALLENGE~ Another challenge was getting detailed and reliable information from the sector.

~RESOLUTION~ BOJ arranged a training seminar/workshop for credit unions on how to prepare prudential data, which is submitted monthly to BOJ for verification/assessment.

~LESSONS LEARNED~

1. I learned the importance of communication, and the need to involve other parties from an early stage, in the decision-making process, in situations in which they are affected, and recognize their views and input.

~HOW TO INTEGRATE YOUR PERSONAL AND PROFESSIONAL LIFE~ I find it very difficult to integrate my personal and professional life because I am involved in several voluntary/outreach activities. I am a very organized person with good administrative skills, so I train my children along the same lines to coordinate our goals and timetables. I start my day early, work late hours, maximize my lunch time by eating at my desk, plan my next day at the end of each work day and I rely on my diary.

In addition, I make time for my family. We eat together on weekends, watch some TV together at nights, do devotions and share our thoughts and feelings in the car in the mornings.

~FORMULA FOR SUCCESS~ Nothing is impossible! Be ambitious, live right, trust God, treat people well, be kind, supportive and understanding, be humble, do not compare yourself to others or envy them for what they have. Others may appear to have everything, but greatly crave and admire what you have and take for granted. We can't be all things to all people. Be yourself, give thanks daily, cherish every moment and be happy as life is a journey and not a destination. I also pattern and use positive, successful and ambitious people as role models.

~MAJOR REGRET~ One of my biggest regrets is that I pushed my children to accept a career of my choice and to be like me instead of being who they wanted to be.

~FAVOURITE QUOTE~ I like "Only the best is good enough" because you can't re-live your life, and one of the worst things is to regret what you could have done, when it's too late.

~INFLUENTIAL BOOK~ Norman Vincent Peale's *The Power of Positive Thinking* and John C. Maxwell's *Your Road Map To Success* had a major impact on my life.

In *The Power of Positive Thinking*, the author talks about the need to put the past behind, focus, treat people right, take time out for oneself, pursue your goals relentlessly and include God in everything you do.

Your Roadmap for Success emphasizes that success is not wealth, power or happiness, and not something one acquires, or achieves, but a journey that you take your whole life. Success is knowing one's purpose in life, how to grow to one's maximum potential and sow seeds that benefit others. The recipe in this book has been the yardstick for measuring the success of my life over the years. I have seen so many so called successful/ accomplished persons who are so miserable and unhealthy to be around I would never want to be identified with their definition of success. The book taught me to live one day at a time and live each day as it were the last.

59

PURDY CRAWFORD
THE WAY TO DO AN ACQUISITION

"If you can keep your head when all about you are losing theirs and blaming it on you."

–Rudyard Kipling

~CHALLENGE~ I've had many business challenges over my long career in law and business, but, the biggest business challenge that I had was when I joined Imasco Limited as CEO in 1985 and we acquired Genstar in 1986 to get Canada Trust. The deal worked well but it was a huge challenge because it was expensive, and risky if we hadn't done the acquisition right.

~ RESOLUTION~ We were successful in the acquisition by getting the right people to run it. We paid $2.5 million for it and sold it to TD Bank in 2002 for $8 million.

60

~LESSONS LEARNED~

1. Have a broad view of things

2. Have a strategy on how you do things, execute the strategy with passion and don't be captivated by investment bankers

~HOW TO INTEGRATE YOUR PERSONAL AND PROFESSIONAL LIFE~ It's hard at times. We have six children and 15 grandchildren. We spend a lot of time with them, though I neglected them somewhat when they were quite young. We attend our grandchildren's hockey and soccer games. Overall, I keep a reasonable perspective. We have a country place where the children come to, and we meet them there.

~FORMULA FOR SUCCESS~ To become successful you have to have a certain amount of intelligence, wisdom, good judgement, fire in your belly, read widely and have a broad perspective on issues.

~MAJOR REGRET~ A major regret is as a young lawyer not being tough enough with clients. I was too accommodating with some of my clients and may have compromised some of my opinions to make them happy.

~FAVOURITE QUOTE~ I like "If you can keep your head when all about you are losing theirs and blaming it on you" from the poem "If" by Rudyard Kipling because it teaches you not to panic and to stay in control when bad things happen. Don't be impulsive and think that you have to do something. Sit in a room for a while and be quiet and let the world go by while you think about things.

Another quote that I like is by a famous European general in World War I and it relates to strategy in business. He said that Generals plan for months on the way they are going to fight the battle and then ten minutes into the battle the plans are useless and those who have the most passion win. This quote is relevant to the business world because everyone talks about the importance of strategy but I talk about the importance of execution.

~INFLUENTIAL BOOK~ I read many books so this is very difficult for me to answer. I like *Alexander Hamilton: The Year That Rocked the World* by Ron Chernow. This book had a major impact on me because it is a biography of an incredible person whom I admire very much. At the age of 13, Alexander Hamilton ran a trading company in the Virgin Islands on behalf of a New York Trading firm, and at 14 he immigrated to the United States. Former Secretary of the Treasury, Hamilton fought in the Revolutionary War with George Washington, created the first financial structure for the United States, and understood the financial structures of the United Kingdom and France. The biography showcases Hamilton's varied life, as well as painting a rich picture of the America that was emerging from the Revolutionary War.

61

NANCI GOVINDER
DOWNSIZING RISKS

"Our deepest fear is not that we are inadequate. Our deepest fear is that we are powerful beyond measure. It is our light, not our darkness that most frightens us. We ask ourselves, "Who am I to be brilliant, gorgeous, talented, fabulous?" Actually, who are you not to be? You are a child of God…"

−Marianne Williamson

~CHALLENGE~ I was part of a management team that was responsible for downsizing a business unit, which included firing a large part of the staff, and relocating the activities of the business unit to another country, with only 12 out of 72 people remaining to support the business unit. We had to show up at a major European medical conference six weeks later as one of the larger exhibitors. We lost product managers with years of experience and the marketing coordinator who was responsible for the exhibition, logistics, hotels and so on.

~RESOLUTION~ I looked around the offices in Europe and the USA for expertise. I pulled salespeople with sound product knowledge out of the field in the US as well as product managers, company veterans to come and help us. The new product managers that were hired in new offices and those that were still working their termination period in their previous jobs took vacation and came to the conference to help out. I explained the severity and urgency of the situation and there was no 'us' versus 'them', which was the perception that prevailed between the country organizations and the Headquarters.

~LESSONS LEARNED~

1. Don't be afraid to show your vulnerability and ask for help

2. If your intention is clear and honest, people will rally around you and unify toward a common goal or vision

3. Don't just focus on short-term costs but rather focus on long-term benefits such as the impact on the brand, customer retention and company image and values

~HOW TO INTEGRATE YOUR PERSONAL AND PROFESSIONAL LIFE~ I do not make distinctions between the two anymore. I have one life—that's it. In my work, I see this separation cause a lot of conflict in people as in: "How can I achieve work-life balance?" The thing is that this does not exist outside of ourselves. Balance or equanimity can only be achieved within oneself.

I take regular breaks in the day to stop, be still and pay attention to my thoughts, feelings and what is going on around me. I pay attention to the voice in my head and question my beliefs at that moment and observe if they are working for or against me.

I, like most professionals, used to spend an awful amount of time being busy and just "doing" in a sleep-walking mode, hoping that the "answer" will miraculously appear. Now, when I lack clarity or focus; I stop, pay attention to what is happening within and around me and the answers emerge.

~FORMULA FOR SUCCESS~ I know that I am being successful at this stage of my life when:

a) I do something everyday that contributes to my personal vision of "Ridding the world of fear"

b) I no longer need external affirmation of my achievements

c) When I stop judging myself and others and accept things for what they are

In a nutshell, it's getting to know who you are and designing and living the life you desire; by overcoming your fears and ridding yourself of the mask you created. When you face the world from a place of self-knowledge and courage, nothing is impossible and nothing will hold you back.

~MAJOR REGRET~ None. I believe that every experience has honed and shaped me to be the person that I am today. I grew up in apartheid South Africa and was oppressed by the government for the major part of my life. People have told me that this is a great story and that I should use it. I don't view it as a "cool" story and don't dwell in the past as the past holds you back. I don't believe in living life looking in the rear view mirror but rather living fully in the present and appreciating and embracing what I have now.

~FAVOURITE QUOTE~ Our Deepest Fear

Our deepest fear is not that we are inadequate, our deepest fear is that we are powerful beyond measure.

It is our light, not our darkness, that most frightens us.

We ask ourselves,

"Who am I to be brilliant, gorgeous, talented and fabulous?"

Actually, who are you not to be?

You are a child of God.

Your playing small does not serve the world.

There is nothing enlightening about shrinking so that other people won't feel insecure around you.

We were born to manifest the glory that is within us.

And as we let our light shine, we unconsciously give other people permission to do the same.

As we are liberated from our own fear, our presence automatically liberates others.

Marianne Williamson, *A Return To Love: Reflections on the Principles of A Course in Miracles,* Harper Collins, 1992. From Chapter 7, Section 3

Nelson Mandela used this quote in his inauguration speech in 1994. It was especially poignant for me as living under apartheid made me feel somewhat diminished and undeserving and this quote really addressed the magnificence that is resident in us all - that every individual has this power and that nothing and nobody could stop me from creating my own reality.

~INFLUENTIAL BOOK~ *That Which You are Seeking is Causing You to Seek* by Cheri Huber made me realize that I no longer needed to go anywhere, do anything, figure anything out or worry about being wrong. This does not imply impassivity, but rather that the answers I sought were not external to me but rather internal. I simplified my life by not worrying about what other people think, stopped comparing myself to others and allowed myself time for pause and reflection. This has given me greater clarity and focus about my life's purpose (helping people develop personal mastery), and inner peace and joy.

CLAIRE HOY
RECOVERING FROM BANKRUPTCY

*Worrying about something is like paying interest on
a debt you don't even know if you owe."* -Mark Twain

~CHALLENGE~ One of the biggest challenges that I faced was when I had
to declare bankruptcy. I never had any money problems until I had
some money. In 1990, I co-authored *By Way of Deception: A Devastating
Insider's Portrait of the Mossad,* a New York Times bestseller, with Victor
Ostrovsky. The book was a huge bestseller and the only Canadian non-
fiction book to be number one on the New York Times Bestseller's List.

With this new money, we invested in several apartment buildings. Our
timing was bad! Bad timing coupled with a lawyer we worked with who
turned out to be a bit dicey, had a gambling problem, and ended up
getting disbarred, forced us to declare bankruptcy.

Being a very public figure and in the media, the bankruptcy was in Frank
magazine. This satirical magazine ran a two-page spread with all the
details of the bankruptcy.

The bankruptcy was a big financial challenge because my children
were still in school, I didn't have a full-time job and there is a stigma
attached.

~RESOLUTION~ You can go to the tallest building and jump off, or you
can carry on and say there it is and get back on your feet and resolve to
make your way through. It took me five to six years to recover. I decided
to work harder since I didn't have a full-time job, and I wrote lots of
columns and more books.

We also reassessed things to determine where we were spending money
and downscaled based on that. In a situation like this, there are two
things that you must do – spend less and bring in more money.

~LESSONS LEARNED~

1. When things appear bleak, you can throw up your hands and jump
   off a tall building or deal with the situation. But, going bankrupt
   isn't that bleak. It's an inconvenience and it doesn't make you feel
   good and your creditors aren't pleased either

continued on next page

65

2. Most people have some skills to offer and just because you made bad investments or had some bad luck, you still have the same skills that got you ahead before. It's like playing golf, which I do a lot of. Just because you had a bad shot in golf doesn't mean that it's the end of the day or the end of your life. You just say that hopefully the next shot will be better

3. I learned that when it comes to financial wizardry I am not very good at it, so now I get the professionals to do it. I focused on my strengths.

~HOW TO INTEGRATE YOUR PERSONAL AND PROFESSIONAL LIFE~ That's a problem. One thing I regret to some extent is that when I was in my first marriage, we had two children and I was just starting out in the business and working my way up, I spent a lot more time at work than I should have. It was only after my first wife died that I realized I had to be at home more because the mother is gone and the children need a father. They were ten and eight years old at the time. That taught me a lesson and it made it very clear to me the importance of being around your family. This is far more important than anything that I might do at work. From that time on I understood the importance of going to your child's ball game or graduation ceremony.

I look back at my father where he and I didn't have a very good relationship. I don't ever remember him taking me anywhere or coming to watch me play hockey, baseball or any of the sports that I played.

Early in my career because I was starting out as a journalist and wanted to be a columnist, at a newspaper, I lost sight of the really important things and lost balance. In the scheme of things the family is more important than work.

Years ago when I was covering Queen's Park and Bill Davis was Premier of Ontario, he went out of his way to be home by 7:00 a.m. to have breakfast with his children because otherwise he wouldn't see them. I learned from that because despite the fact that he had a busy job he realized that there was more to life than being Premier of Ontario and having the kind of power that comes with it. This was a good life lesson for me.

~FORMULA FOR SUCCESS~ First you have to decide what success is. I consider myself very successful in my life now. I am not wealthy beyond my wildest dreams, but I love my life. I have five healthy children who are happy and doing well. My partner is happy and doing well and I think that's successful. I get to play golf four times a week, I work at home, write and do radio and television stuff and get to do the kinds of things that I love to do. And, the best thing is that I do not have to do it at anybody else's behest.

Most people look at success in economic or status terms, but I look at success in terms of doing what you like, and enjoying the lifestyle that comes about. So many people get so wrapped up in the traditional view of success such as getting to the top so that all the other things that are not part of that get left out. No one on their deathbeds ever said that they wished that they had spent more time at the office. People say I wished I had spent more time with the children, playing golf, going to the opera and whatever it is that they do.

~MAJOR REGRET~ It's really funny because I have had some regrets and setbacks in life, but it's always been my attitude not to dwell on them. My first wife died from cancer at 33 years old and we had two young children. I wish that hadn't happened. There is nothing I could do about it. That was the way it was. I split up with my second wife. I was fired about six times from various jobs, and I had to declare bankruptcy. All these things are regretful, but I just do not dwell on them. I just do not have one single thing that is a major regret.

67

If I look back on my life and everything that has happened, I can't really say that I would have done anything differently from what I have done. I don't dwell on things that went badly, I tend to look forward and say that everyone has good and bad things happen to them.

I know people, and I am sure you do too, who dwell on all the bad things that happen to them and end up being so sour. I remember years ago when I was working for the Toronto Star, we had great difficulty ideologically and I ended up getting fired and that was a very good thing because I wasn't happy there and I probably wouldn't have left on my own accord. It's the only job I have ever had where I hated going in, in the mornings. I was grumpy with the people around me because I hated the job so much. At the time I was regretting having that job, but when I was looking back, I realized that I was turning into one of those people who was moaning and groaning all the time. I didn't like that because it was the only time in my life when I had fallen into that and it convinced me not to do it again.

Ever since then, I have turned down things that I could have made money on. People who are sitting in their offices at 10:00 p.m. trying to finish a report that is so important, should ask themselves if five years from now if they are going to have any recollection of what was so important about the report. Your children will always be important.

I constantly remind myself of these sorts of things and that's how I keep a balance in my life.

Not keeping a balance leaves your children without a father or mother figure and it gives the impression that the family isn't important, which leads to break-ups in relationships.

~FAVOURITE QUOTE~ I like "Worrying about something is like paying interest on a debt you don't even know if you owe" by Mark Twain and "It ain't over till it's over" by Yogi Berra because I view them as great life lessons. In Mark Twain's case he is saying that if you are going around and worrying and fretting how badly something is going to turn out, almost all the time it never turns out as badly as you perceived. In Berra's case, if you don't throw up your hands when things go wrong, but think it isn't over and that you still have a chance, anything is possible. For me bankruptcy wasn't the end of the world, it looked bad but I got through it.

~INFLUENTIAL BOOK~ *The New Testament* has been my moral compass and when I have had serious problems I learned from it. It shaped the way that I try to conduct my life. Whenever I have heavy personal issues I reach for it. My moral values are based on *The New Testament*. It is the runaway winner for influencing my life. There are life lessons in the context of teaching you something. It is filled with people facing all kinds of adversities and how to deal with them.

AMELIA KASSEL
CHANGING YOUR MARKETING STRATEGY

"There is nothing to fear but fear itself."
-Franklin D. Roosevelt

~CHALLENGE~ I started my business in 1982, and in 1984, co-founded my current business, MarketingBase, with two other strategic partners. In 1986, I took over the business. At the time, a big transition was to go from using networking as the major marketing initiative, to direct marketing. I adapted and changed directions to integrate a different target market into my business through the application of an entirely different marketing strategy. Over the years, I have changed directions a few times. Each has been a new challenge that I've integrated into my work life successfully.

~RESOLUTION~ Implement new marketing programs, assess how they work, and improve them until effective.

~LESSONS LEARNED~

1. You can make change effectively
2. At a business level, there is always risk, but you can take the risk and follow your intuition
3. It's very satisfying when you make a change and succeed

~HOW TO INTEGRATE YOUR PERSONAL AND PROFESSIONAL LIFE~ It is very rewarding to experiment with new ideas and programs and succeed at them. It is a powerful incentive to go in new directions when it seems important. My business is a creative process that I find personally satisfying.

~FORMULA FOR SUCCESS~ The four Ds: Determination, discipline, dedication, and drive. Plus, you have to be able to experiment and try new things, take risks, and when something doesn't work out the way you expected, do not view it as failure, but as a learning experience. You learn from trial and error and by how you reshape things.

69

~ MAJOR REGRET~ I cannot think of any major regret. I started a business because I wanted to remain in the beautiful California wine country where I had resided for 10 years and at the same time become involved with new and intellectually stimulating challenges. I have done everything that I set out to do, and more, and created a worldwide research and consulting firm. I also teach what I have learned in an email-based training program for others starting in this field and last year began teaching courses to graduate students via distance education.

~FAVOURITE QUOTE~ I like "There is nothing to fear but fear itself" by Franklin D. Roosevelt because it's so easy to feel fear when you are starting a new business or taking risks . In life, you face many situations where it's easy to feel fearful. This quote reminds me that I can do things that I wouldn't otherwise try.

~INFLUENTIAL BOOK~ I take my strength from inside of me. Since I was named after Amelia Earhart, I was inspired by her pioneering life and by the lives of immigrants and others who meet unique challenges or make contributions to the lives of others. These stories have been my guiding lights.

ANN KIRKLAND
BUSINESS TRANSFER AS A MEANS TO EXPAND

"...Find that place where your deep gladness meets the world's deep need." -Frederick Beuchner

~CHALLENGE~ I started my business in 1998 while I was still working. Since I gave up my full-time job, my business has grown, but not as big, or as fast as I would like, but still too big for me to manage by myself. I was finding myself being absolutely overwhelmed with work and it was taking the fun out of it. I was also spending too much of my time selling, doing finance and a lot of administrative functions, all things that I didn't like or wasn't good at.

I just turned sixty so I figured that I have at least five years left before retirement. I knew that eventually I would want to see this business continue, independent of me, and I would also like to sell it.

My challenge was to keep the business going and growing while I was able to reduce the amount of time that I was spending on administrative things, and be able to effectively transfer the business to someone else. All the value in my business is intellectual property. It's my ideas that I would be selling.

71

I have been working with a travel company because by law I cannot offer trips. I need certain types of insurance and regulatory memberships and things that I do not have, so I had to team up with a travel company.

~RESOLUTION~ About 18 months ago we started working together. I can't even remember who suggested a purchase of my business. We both decided to take it slowly and agreed to work together for a year, where I wouldn't give them my mailing list or processes for doing things. They would simply book the trips as I requested and take registrations. This took a tremendous burden off me, but we weren't working as effectively together as we could. After a year of doing the partnership successfully, we both felt comfortable with each other. They wanted to buy and I wanted to sell, but I didn't want to stop working either. To take full advantage of the opportunity I realized that I would have to give them all of the intellectual property now. We worked out an agreement where they would take ownership of the company, it would stay in my name and be invisible to others because a lot of the credibility comes from name recognition and association with me, and they would still allow me to call most of the shots. They would do the things they do well that I do not like to do.

My financial advisor recommended an accountant who does business transfers and we made an offer but the travel agency didn't go for it. After a few rounds of negotiation, we asked them to make an offer. The offer was lower than what I would have wanted, but after more negotiation they made some of the changes to suit me.

The sale will take away the kind of risk that I have been living with for the past few years. For example, I had a trip to New Orleans in November 2005, and there was a huge cost involved. When hurricane Katrina struck, the trip was cancelled and I had to refund everyone's money. This wasn't a breakeven situation for me because I was out thousands of dollars. I will escape all these risks and the travel agency will now assume all the risks.

I will have a steadier income. It's not a big income but a secure one and I think that I will be able to quit my working life on a more reasonable basis.

~LESSONS LEARNED~

1. You always have to stop and think longer term. You also have to take time to lift your head from the day-to-day work and ask where you want to be in a year, two years and five years. Think about what's working well and what's not working so well, what you enjoy doing, what you don't enjoy doing and find some people to talk to. As long as you keep doing the same things day after day the new ideas aren't going to come

2. Know that you often have to spend money to get from here to there

3. You have to be patient because it always takes longer than you think

4. Be flexible! Even though you have a goal of where you want to go, you have to realize that you may have to alter it in some way as you go, and try to be as clear as you can be about which things are important to hold firm on and which to let go

~HOW TO INTEGRATE YOUR PERSONAL AND PROFESSIONAL LIFE~ By changing what I do for a living it's a more thorough integration of my personal and professional life. When I worked in healthcare I made some friends at work and I was interested in what I did, but there was a much clearer demarcation of work and personal life and generally my personal interests were different from my professional interests. My friends were different and just the fact that I was going out to work was clear when I was at work and when I wasn't. Now, that's all blurred and it's mostly a good thing. I am not one of those people who will get up, put on makeup and sit down and say okay it's 9:00 a.m. the workday begins and turns off the computer at 6:00 p.m.

Every time that I am out doing something around town or anywhere else I've got an antenna saying is there anything here that will be useful for me for my summer program, or for travel? The one part that I don't like doing is the selling. If someone knows about what I do and comes to me, I am happy to talk all day long about what I do. Hustling is not one of my strengths. Every book that I read, every concert I go to, everything seems linked and I like that, so I am happy to have that blurring of boundaries.

~FORMULA FOR SUCCESS~ I certainly do not know how I would define success, but I would certainly do, what I have done again. The great satisfaction or the great key for anyone is finding your own personal vocation. There is no guarantee that if you find it, it's going to work, but I think that finding something that incorporates who you are, your own personal nature with something that feels worthwhile is very satisfying. Most of us have a need to feel like we are making a contribution, making a difference. Knowing who you are and what your gifts are, your limitations, and then finding a way to put that to use that is a benefit to the world, somehow helps. You also need to know what your energy level is, knowing what help you need and going out there to get it. Don't think that you can figure it out all by yourself. Know what to hold firm on and where to be flexible. You also need to take breaks to refresh yourself. The whole idea of a sabbatical is very important and I wish it was built into everybody's work, but it isn't, but I think people have to take it. When you work for yourself it's very hard to even take a weekend let alone a week when you're not getting paid and don't even know where the next money is coming from. The other thing is being some combination of being realistic and idealistic. You have to realize that the world that you live in, has constraints, whether it is cultural, financial or whatever. You have to work within these constraints and push the boundaries and be as imaginative and creative as you can. You have to find a match between your own nature and something that is needed in the world.

73

~MAJOR REGRET~ I have kids and my biggest regret is not having a lifelong happy marriage. I have been divorced twice and I have been divorced now for 20 years. I have good relationships with two former husbands so I don't know whether it was a mistake marrying each of them in the first instance or it was a mistake to leave them one after the other. I don't know, but that is a deep regret that I have.

~FAVOURITE QUOTE~ I like the discussion about vocation: "Find that place where your deep gladness and the world's deep hunger meet" by Frederick Beuchner because it combines that intersection of "selfhood" and "service," and that tension that I have often felt between saying oh if I do this thing it's selfish and or if I do that thing it doesn't feel right, and it's realizing that both "selfhood" and "service" have to be in harmony for life to be fulfilling and worthwhile. We all have strengths and weaknesses, likes and dislikes, and thankfully the world needs lots of different things. The world needs people to be friendly and helpful; people to help others cross the streets, people to sit in a lab and design engines or whatever. What's important is that we recognize and celebrate our differences.

~INFLUENTIAL BOOK~ *Divine Comedy*, a book about a man who takes his midlife crisis very seriously by Dante Alighieri, is a book I could read for many years and take on a deserted island. Written in the 1300s, it is a very complex book that can be read on many different levels, and it helps to have other people to discuss it with. The man starts out being on a path, which he gets off - he gets lost in the woods. He sees a hill with the sun up there and thinks he can climb up the hill and everything will be fine. But, as he is climbing up the hill he encounters three beasts, a lion, leopard and wolf that chases him back down the hill, and he realizes that he has to go back down through the inferno and up through purgatory until he reaches paradise. It is written on a beautiful poetic level, a metaphoric level, a spiritual level, a political level and I love it because the man takes it seriously. He is introspective, he is looking out at the world, he is trying to figure out who he is and he realizes that the world isn't all about just me, me, me, and I want, I want, but there is an obligation attached to it that brings joy. He takes seriously his yearnings for God, for a deeply religious life, but he doesn't take as given, everything that has been handed down to him. He's a huge questioner. To me, *Divine Comedy* is an incredibly inspiring book to give place and room in my life for longings that I've had, but pushed away, but now, I have given much more prominence in my life.

74

SEATON MCLEAN
KNOW WHERE YOU'RE DRIVING

"An investment in knowledge always pay the best interest."
-Benjamin Franklin

~CHALLENGE~ There are two major challenges that I would like to talk about. The first occurred when the company went public in 1993 and had to redefine itself from being a closely-knit family run business to having to deal with shareholders and conduct its business in a way to meet the expectations of all stakeholders.

The second challenge occurred in 2003 when I had to downsize the production area of the company over a two-year time period. Two hundred people lost their jobs, which was very emotional. It was extremely hard to maintain morale when you conduct layoffs over a period of time and are constantly saying goodbyes. It's difficult for the people who remain because they know that ultimately they are going to lose their jobs as well. It was difficult for me but I had to put the emotional connection aside and let people go or let the company struggle financially. The downsizing process was a factor in my decision to leave the company after so many years.

~RESOLUTION~ I had to look down the road to where we wanted the company to be before I took the first step. The resolution is where you are driving.

~LESSONS LEARNED~

1. In both situations, there was a larger life lesson; as long as you are honest you can resolve 99 percent of all situations amicably and without regret

2. Stay true to yourself and do not change your beliefs, philosophies or approach just to get ahead

~HOW TO INTEGRATE YOUR PERSONAL AND PROFESSIONAL LIFE~ I do not make a distinction because they are one and the same. Over the years, I have changed the proportion of time I spent working and the time I spent on my personal life. When I was single, my friends were my coworkers and I worked everyday. When I married, I would work only one day of the weekend and when we had our daughter, I stopped working weekends.

75

My wife and I work in the same industry, so do our friends, so work inevitably comes up at dinners and cocktail parties. Looking back, as my life changed over the years, I made adjustments to accommodate the changes.

~**FORMULA FOR SUCCESS**~ If I knew the formula for success I would bottle it. Whenever I mentored people, they always wanted to know what I did to become successful so that they could replicate the success. I would always tell my mentees that the elements in place and the stars are now aligned differently so they shouldn't try to be me, but instead be themselves.

If there is any advice that I would give about the formula for success is to be tenacious, never say I give up or that things are not happening fast enough. Have a goal in mind that you want to achieve, set your goal very high and be able to communicate your idea. If you cannot communicate you will be hard pressed to succeed.

~**MAJOR REGRET**~ I do not have any major regrets. I consider myself lucky and cannot think of any major thing in my life that I would have done differently.

~**FAVOURITE QUOTE**~ I like "An investment in knowledge always pay the best interest" by Benjamin Franklin and have had it in front of me for the last 20 years. I believe that if a society invests in knowledge it will have a common base to communicate. We as individuals also have to put the emotional investment into educating ourselves so that we can put things in perspective, read between the lines and understand how certain issues such as racism and poverty impact all of us.

~**INFLUENTIAL BOOK**~ I read a lot of books and I like science fiction. The books, which impacted me, include *Slaughterhouse-Five* by Kurt Vonnegut, books by Ray Bradbury. In addition, a seminal moment for me was when I read *Lord of the Rings* as a teenager.

JIM ROHN
HOW TO RETURN TO PROFITABILITY

"Nothing can resist a human will that will stake even its existence on the extent of its purpose."

-Benjamin Disraeli

~CHALLENGE~ In the early 1980s I had 13 satellite offices, all filled with people working hard, but we were losing money. A number of advisors said that we should open more offices and the result would be that we would then make money. I disagreed. I figured that if we opened more offices, we would just be compounding the losses. At this point I was faced with a difficult decision, but difficult decisions are one of the skills necessary and often what leadership is about.

~RESOLUTION~ Strong leadership is required, at times, to make hard decisions. So I pulled the plug. We were already doing all that we could yet it wasn't enough to make a profit using the strategy of satellite offices. We finally took our number of satellite offices down to only two -- the groups that were the strongest and most profitable. Then we went back to the basics and worked to become profitable again. I still remember the pain of that hard decision, because it affected so many people. By some, it could be perceived as failure, but for us it was a strategic decision that had to be made to make our company viable and successful for the long-term. And here we are decades later, more profitable than ever. Challenges like those that I faced are hard, but when you face them head on with courage, integrity and faith, you will be ahead of the game in the long run.

77

~LESSONS LEARNED~

1. The only way to survive in business is to be profitable, unless you have an unlimited amount of money

2. Get through your difficulty and learn to do better next time

~HOW TO INTEGRATE YOUR PERSONAL AND PROFESSIONAL LIFE~ Integrating
my personal life and professional life has always been a challenge. It's difficult to keep family, friends, social and work all in balance. You have to recognize the challenges and develop a plan. Do not ignore them. Now that I am older, I do less work and have more time for charity. When I

was younger, I constantly had to negotiate with family and friends. I paid attention to the challenges.

~**FORMULA FOR SUCCESS**~ You have to understand the philosophy of success. You have to be helpful to the marketplace and find a product or service that adds value. I like what Zig Ziglar says, "You can have everything in life you want if you will just help enough other people get what they want."

To be successful there are two values that you bring to the table. They are:

1. The product or service

2. The value that you become

The more valuable you become, the more influence you have, the better communicator you are, you manage your time better, and you recognize people for their contributions. You also become more valuable as a spouse, parent and friend.

In addition, to be successful, you have to develop certain traits such as courage, dignity, charisma and integrity. You also have to recognize that you have to work harder on yourself than on your job. You attract success because of the person you are. Personal development is key.

Find partners to work with because no one succeeds alone.

For economic safety for the future, you must have multiple skills and languages. Success is basically being the best that you can be.

~**MAJOR REGRET**~ No regrets! I've been blessed with a unique life -- from childhood up until now. If I did have any, they are all gone by now -- they've disappeared from my memory.

~**FAVOURITE QUOTE**~ I like "Nothing can resist a human will that will stake even its existence on the extent of its purpose" by Benjamin Disraeli because it challenges the human spirit to ultimate possibility – give it all you've got. Become all you were designed to become. It simply means do it or die. We all need challenges.

~**INFLUENTIAL BOOK**~ I always read *The Holy Bible* and it's the one book that has had the biggest impact on me. It is filled with history, poetry and excellent love stories. It gives key advice to follow.

DONALD WILLIAMS
DESIGNING A NEW SYSTEM

" Labour for learning before you grow old, for learning is better than silver and gold. Silver and gold will vanish away, but a good education will never decay."
Popular Jamaican Proverb

~CHALLENGE~ The biggest business challenge that I have ever had occurred about three years ago when I was given the full responsibility to design, document and implement a new credit system to "Retailise" the small business credit/loans within the entire Bank of Nova Scotia Jamaica Limited.

At the time, all loan applications were prepared manually throughout the bank after credit officers gathered information from customers. For each loan, you needed:

- The latest financial statements prepared in accordance with a prescribed format, and personal financial statements of the guarantor(s), usually the principal(s)

- The history and management report on the business; and an application/advise for credit in the prescribed format

If the credit officer had the signing authority to approve the amount of the loan, the loan would be processed at the branch, otherwise, the loan applicant would have to go to the head office.

This process was bureaucratic, cumbersome, inefficient and unproductive. We couldn't service our clients in a timely manner because the process was so onerous. The industry wasn't as competitive as it should be, and we all had to reduce the paper work to meet customers' needs, our targets to book loans while seeking to manage risks.

~RESOLUTION~ I received help from a special department set up in the head office of Scotiabank in Toronto, Canada. We formed a committee to design, document and implement the programme across the branch network. The following plan was drafted and agreed on:

- Conduct research at bank level

- Conduct focus groups made up of senior and experienced managers

- Identify and contract resource personnel from Texas, USA to design a Scoring System to meet the bank's special needs

79

- Prepare a business case to include funding and staffing needs, period of implementation, short and long-term objectives

- Establish a management group, both in Jamaica and Toronto

  - We met every Wednesday morning at 10:00 a.m. and agreed on an action plan. Each member of the group was given specific tasks with timelines attached

After we designed the computer system we were ready to implement it. We trained 120 credit staff across the bank, explained what the changes were and what it would mean, and outlined the benefits and costs to both themselves as well as to the bank.

We decided to use a classroom-training format, and with the aid of my co-workers in Canada, we started the training using PowerPoint. Mid way through the training, there was an outbreak of the " SARS Epidemic" across the world and this curtailed travel from certain countries, including people from North America. As a result of this development, we had to find alternatives because we could not stop the programme in mid-stream.

At this stage, some secondary challenges emerged. Three critical issues surfaced:

1. Curtailed travel caused a pause in training and extended the project

2. Credit staff was hesitant and unsure of the process, so the use of the system was almost nil

3. Lending severely curtailed because the old system was disbanded for small loans below Jam $4,000,000

~RESOLUTION~

- Continued the training by using WebEx

- Hired nine contract workers, trained them, and sent them into the field to train the regular credit staff

- Coached staff on how to use the new system, provided prompt responses to their loan requests, and sold them on the benefits of using the system

Though the challenges were difficult to resolve, the process was very rewarding.

Today we process work for all the Caribbean branches and we make decisions for over 6,500,000 loan requests per month. The project was awarded third place in the Bank of Nova Scotia system, the year that it was implemented.

~LESSONS LEARNED~

1. Through hard work, perseverance and dedication, there is nothing that I cannot do or hurdle too high that I cannot overcome

~HOW TO INTEGRATE YOUR PERSONAL AND PROFESSIONAL LIFE~ I schedule
time for family, friends and recreation. Simply put, one must create a balance. Pray without ceasing as prayer conquers all.

~FORMULA FOR SUCCESS~ I think that the formula for success is to get a good education because education opens doors. It is the poor man's passport to a better quality of life.

~MAJOR REGRET~ A major regret that I have, is that I did not study harder when I was younger. I also regret that I did not embrace the game of lawn tennis when I was younger and more agile.

~FAVOURITE QUOTE~ I like '' Labour for learning before you grow old, for learning is better than silver and gold. Silver and gold will vanish away, but a good education will never decay."

~INFLUENTIAL BOOK~ *The Entrepreneurial Journey in Jamaica: When Policies Derail* by Dr. Paul Chen-Young had a profound impact on me because I was an employee of a large Multinational Commercial Bank [Canadian in origin] that had operated in Jamaica for almost 100 years. I had significant exposure and training on good corporate governance, and, at the time when the financial debacle was unfolding, I questioned my exposure and training given to me over the years, as also the BANK'S focus. The book had a very positive impact on me because it confirmed that my training and exposure over the years were correct, and that good financial management would always redound to one's benefit, whether or not it is practised personally, by a corporation or by our government.

81

82

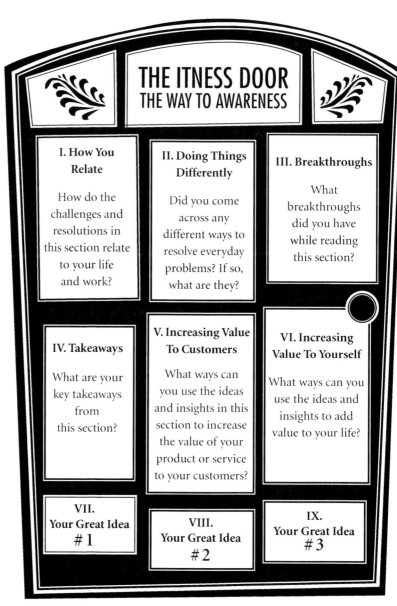

THE ITNESS DOOR
THE WAY TO AWARENESS

I. How You Relate

How do the challenges and resolutions in this section relate to your life and work?

II. Doing Things Differently

Did you come across any different ways to resolve everyday problems? If so, what are they?

III. Breakthroughs

What breakthroughs did you have while reading this section?

IV. Takeaways

What are your key takeaways from this section?

V. Increasing Value To Customers

What ways can you use the ideas and insights in this section to increase the value of your product or service to your customers?

VI. Increasing Value To Yourself

What ways can you use the ideas and insights to add value to your life?

VII. Your Great Idea #1

VIII. Your Great Idea #2

IX. Your Great Idea #3

83

84

QUOTABLES

Work/Life balance is a myth. Work and Life are completely integrated.
~Gail Blanke

I live what I do and I am doing who I am. ~Peter Bouffard

We can't be all things to all people. Be yourself, give thanks daily, cherish every moment and be happy as life is a journey and not a destination. ~Prudence Brown

Success is the awareness in each moment of who you ARE and the celebration of your Unfolding as you go through your life, regardless of changing circumstances. ~Lea Chambers

It's important to understand what's in people's minds, and separate it from what they are actually saying and discussing with their peers. ~Arunas Chesonis

Know that everything happens for a reason. Once you signal to the universe where you are going, you just need to let go and allow things to unfold. ~Samy Chong

If you are true to yourself, it is easy to be true to others... Just be as authentically YOU as you can be in all situations. ~Lydia Danner

The formula for success is remaining angry and never forgetting what it is that makes you want to get up in the morning, never losing your edge and not getting too comfortable. ~Gabriel Draven

If you focus on the goals, you will make your bosses happy, but you sell yourself short – life, love, and work are all a series of journeys. Goals happen, are temporary and then are gone and leave emptiness. ~Simon Grant

If you don't throw up your hands when things go wrong, but think it isn't over and that you still have a chance, anything is possible. ~Claire Hoy

The whole idea of a sabbatical is very important and I wish it was built into everybody's work. ~Ann Kirkland

You really do need to surround yourself with good people, and recognize that you cannot do anything by yourself... You need to have people around you who complement what you bring because your own weaknesses are made irrelevant by other people's strength. ~Gloria Lattanzio

Be prepared to accept that people may not be as ready as you are to move forward or to take leaps of faith. ~Janice Lawrence-Clarke

As long as you are honest you can resolve 99 percent of all situations amicably and without regret. ~Seaton McLean

I measure my success not against others, but by my own progress in overcoming day-to-day challenges, continuously learning and growing from those experiences. ~Asha McLeod

You need a support structure in place to check in with you, encourage you and give you the courage to go on. ~Maria Nemeth

When you are poor you do not need bags of money to sustain yourself. It's when you are rich that you do! ~Anthea Rossouw

Small steps daily will take you further ahead of people with lofty goals who do nothing. ~Chris Widener

[Education] is the poor man's passport to a better quality of life. ~Donald Williams

86

"Things go wrong that I regret, but when I look back with perspective I do not ever regret anything." -Suzanne Gibson

"I believe that every experience has honed and shaped me to be the person that I am today." -Nanci Govinder

"It's really funny because I have had some regrets and setbacks in life, but it's always been my attitude not to dwell on them." ~Claire Hoy

"You always think about what might have been, but I have learned to go with the cards that I have been dealt." -Andrea Nierenberg

"I do not have any major regrets. I consider myself lucky and cannot think of any major thing in my life that I would have done differently." ~Seaton McLean

"No regrets! I've been blessed with a unique life -- from childhood up until now." ~Jim Rohn

"All of life comes with its highs and its lows. It's not possible to have your highs without your lows." ~Tonya Lee Williams

SECTION 2
PART 3: INNOVATION

STEPHEN ABRAM

ARUNAS CHESONIS

GABRIEL DRAVEN

SUZANNE GIBSON

JANICE LAWRENCE-CLARKE

JOSEPH MARTIN

ANTHEA ROSSOUW

STEPHEN ABRAM
SEEING THINGS DIFFERENTLY

"Eternity is a mere moment, just long enough for a
joke even if it is sardonic."

-Hermann Hesse

~CHALLENGE~ I work for a software solutions company that provides software to many libraries in North America. The biggest challenge that I face is understanding the marketplace in which our firm operates. We collect lots of data, and we harvest data from our client servers. We know what's happening in libraries across North America. We know what the users in libraries are doing, but we also want to know why they are doing it.

~RESOLUTION~ We conducted focus group interviews of hundreds of library end-users, using the Cynefin process to identify what they are trying to achieve and what their unique needs are. This process provided only a partial picture so we also collected hundreds of stories from librarians to understand and identify the gap between what they are ultimately trying to achieve and what their users' needs are. We are using a sophisticated software to drill down into the data to find psychological patterns in stories, and develop profiles. Ultimately our aim is to build library systems around the end-user, to make our clients more successful, which will make us more successful.

~LESSONS LEARNED~

1. Problems are often complex and you need to find a multifaceted solution

2. You need to look at things from different dimensions

~HOW TO INTEGRATE YOUR PERSONAL AND PROFESSIONAL LIFE~ Your personal and professional life is one and the same because you have one life. I have a high level position at my company, which keeps me very busy. I am away a lot traveling on business – about 20-25 days a month. I am a writer with several periodical columns and articles due monthly. I teach at the University, and I also give 60 to 70 speeches each year to conferences around the world. Because of that, my personal life is

88

pretty intense. I have a wife and two older children. I would say that my personal and professional life is integrated but not balanced.

~FORMULA FOR SUCCESS~ The formula for success is listening, asking questions and continuous learning.

~MAJOR REGRET~ Probably not doing my PhD, I would really love to do that. If I won a million dollars today, the first thing that I would do is my PhD.

~FAVOURITE QUOTE~ I like "Eternity is a mere moment, just long enough for a joke even if it is sardonic" by Hermann Hesse because your life sometimes serves as a warning to others. Often, people are too serious. Sometimes you laugh and other times you should just see the irony in the situation.

~INFLUENTIAL BOOK~ A book, which had a profound impact on me, is *The Gift: The Form and Reason for Exchange in Archaic Societies* by Marcel Mauss, a social anthropologist. It talks about the role of gift giving in society and how stories are gifts. You help people through gifts, and the library's role is gifting to the community or to the learner.

ARUNAS CHESONIS
TREATING EMPLOYEES FAIRLY

"Us surrender? Aw, nuts!" -General McAuliffe

~**CHALLENGE**~ When we were starting the company, we wanted to make sure that the first one hundred founders of the company felt that they were owners of the business. When you are raising money in multiple rounds of financing, it is very difficult to be aware that your stocks are going to get diluted down. How were we going to make people feel comfortable that they were going to be treated fairly through the multiple rounds of financing that we were contemplating?

~**RESOLUTION**~ We came up with a straight percentage ownership that their offer letter said they would get after the third round of financing. This made people more comfortable, and that's when we started accelerating the hiring process and ended up hiring 71 of the 75 people we interviewed in the first three months.

90

~LESSONS LEARNED~

1. It is very important to address the issues that are impacting people's decision-making – you have to try to extract the issues from them. In the initial interviews and meetings the stock option wasn't coming out as a significant issue

2. It's important to understand what's in people's minds, and separate it from what they are actually saying and discussing with their peers

~**HOW TO INTEGRATE YOUR PERSONAL AND PROFESSIONAL LIFE**~ I usually work from 7:30 a.m. to 5:00 p.m. during the week and go two nights a week on average to conferences and trips to other regional offices for the company. On the weekends, unless I am travelling, I turn off the cell phone and blackberry and just spend time with my family and decompress. This keeps me from burning out.

~**FORMULA FOR SUCCESS**~ You have to understand that for most people the most important thing in life for them is not their career or job, but their family and life outside your company. Once you keep that in the front of your thinking, you can make sure that you run your business properly because most people if they had nest eggs, or were wealthy wouldn't be doing what they are doing in your company. They are working for you to pay for other parts of their lives. If you treat people better, treat them with respect, be flexible concerning their family and health concerns, and pay them what they are worth, this will be a motivating factor for them and this is the formula for success.

~MAJOR REGRET~ When we started PAETEC seven years ago, my sister and my brother moved to Rochester. When all three children moved, my parents moved here as well and I guess my biggest regret is not having my family living closer to me sooner. After high school we lived in separate cities for seventeen years.

~FAVOURITE QUOTE~ My favourite quote is "NUTS" by General McAuliffe. On December 22, 1944 during the "Battle of the Bulge," the Germans had totally surrounded the American forces 101st Airborne Division at Bastogne and issued a surrender ultimatum. When General McAuliffe heard about the ultimatum he laughed and said: "Us surrender? Aw, nuts!" He then sent the written response "To the German Commander, Nuts! A.C. McAuliffe, Commanding." Col. Harper who delivered the message to the Germans explained, "If you don't know what "Nuts" means, in plain English it is the same as Go to Hell."

91

Between General McAuliffe's reply, Patton's troops from the south, and a change in the weather that allowed air reinforcement the following day, the 101st was able to hold Bastogne. Their victory resulted in the first full-Division Presidential Distinguished Unit Citation.

I like the Phrase "NUTS" because it shows that even when things look their bleakest you can still come out on top.

~INFLUENTIAL BOOK~ It wasn't so much a book that had a profound impact on me but a course taught by Mike Jensen at Rochester University in the late 1980s. The course, "Rules of the Game" talked about the rules of the game, how you set up different compensation programs for different employees, how setting up the rules actually affect people's behaviour, and if you can set-up those rules in such a way to benefit the company as well as the employees, that is make them aligned, you'll be more successful as an organization. I use these thoughts in different areas of my life. There were many books that were a part of this course, but this is the basic concept.

GABRIEL DRAVEN
LIVING AN AUTHENTIC LIFE

*"To succeed in life, you need two things:
ignorance and confidence."* -Mark Twain

~CHALLENGE~ My biggest business challenge was learning how to live authentically in the workplace. I spent 10 years in the corporate world in an environment that just didn't suit me. By the time I was 35 years old, I am 40 now, I had spent 10 years in the workplace, and was in about the 95th percentile in terms of income. At the end of the day, I was asking myself what I had accomplished for the day, and I was getting madder and madder, and it was a real challenge to me to spend the next 30 years of my life doing work that doesn't really make any kind of difference. The work didn't feed my soul and I was working with people who I didn't have anything in common with. How do I actually begin to live authentically and make a living authentically? This was the biggest challenge that I have ever faced. And, quite frankly, I got laid off one day when the dotcom implosion happened and I said well I can find another job, in which case I'll be in the same position that I am in now, or I can use this as an opportunity to springboard into going independent and do my own thing.

I decided to use my layoff as an opportunity to do my own thing. I am still in that process right now. It was really tough to make the transition from working for someone and being unhappy, to becoming an independent and living authentically.

~RESOLUTION~ How did I do it? I just did it. I threw all my money at it; I threw all my work and effort at it. Over a period of 4 years it began to work its way out. Essentially, it was a 4-year transition.

~SECONDARY CHALLENGE~ When the dotcom implosion occurred, I decided that I would do consulting work in the technology field and use it as a stepping-stone to do more. First, all my clients lost their businesses. My contacts were on the eastern seaboard of the United States and then September 11th happened. The entire regional economy that I was targeting basically imploded. There was a trillion dollar meltdown in the stock market, you had 9/11 happen and what you saw was the first downturn in the consulting sector since the 1970s. All this happened the same month I decided to become an independent consultant. I tried to take a few corrective courses of action, but again,

92

most of my contacts were on the eastern seaboard of the United States. I was working in Connecticut and living in Toronto. The industry, which I operated in, was decimated.

All these factors contributed to the transition taking so long.

~RESOLUTION~ I had the courage of my convictions. I have talent, a very good track record, and I recognized that it was a matter of just going out there and do it.

I have worked in companies, and around the water cooler, I would get together with people who hated their jobs and they would say, "One day I am going to leave." One person wanted to open a clothing store, and another wanted to open a flower shop. I worked with entire floors of people who were completely disengaged from their jobs and wanted to do something else with their lives. Five years later they are still doing the same things.

To me, there wasn't so much a grand strategy, but pure brute force. I had to leave. I didn't want to be saying four years later that I "shoulda" or "coulda." I decided to just do it. I am very good at strategy. I graduated very high in my class in my MBA program. I was co-awarded Schulich School of Business' top award for strategy studies in 2001. Though I am good at strategy, there comes a time where you have to pull the trigger.

93

~LESSONS LEARNED~

1. If you want to make it happen, just go out and do it

2. You have to be prepared to bet the farm and if you're not prepared to bet the farm, do not play this game.

~HOW TO INTEGRATE YOUR PERSONAL AND PROFESSIONAL LIFE~
It took me about five years to figure this out. I have a solid 10 years of corporate experience in brand management, but I was also very involved in environmental politics, so it took me a number of years to figure out how to marry these two things. I am now launching a renewable energy financing company. As we are seeing energy prices increase, I have figured out a business model to sell, rent and lease solar heating systems and geothermal heating and cooling systems - renewable energy systems.

I had to try and figure out how to integrate my personal value set with a way to make money, and I finally did it. Part of it was serendipity, part of it was chance, and part of it was pure thinking. So I am now in the fortunate position where I am retired at the age of 40. By conventional definition I work 12, 13, 14, 15 hours each day, but to me it isn't work. I have finally figured out a way to make money doing what I love. I never want to retire. I want to be like Peter Drucker. I personally can't ever see myself retiring.

~FORMULA FOR SUCCESS~ Anthony Robbins has made millions of dollars doing seminars on the formula for success. You have to keep going out there and try to make your dreams happen. Most people give up on their dreams. They get locked into this comfortable place that's not so comfortable. They find themselves making a reasonable income, so they've got bronze handcuffs on, and they find themselves buying things with that income, and it's a trap. This has become their life, and they keep forgetting how much they actually hate it and how unauthentic it is.

The formula for success to me is, remaining angry and never forgetting what it is that makes you want to get up in the morning, never losing your edge and not getting too comfortable.

94

I know people who live in wonderful houses, they constantly go on trips, they've got cars, they've got all the shit that we say makes them successful, but they are a couple of pay cheques away from insolvency. They couldn't leave their jobs now even if they wanted to, because it would mean getting rid of all that stuff. Not many people are prepared to get rid of their stuff. It gets to the point where their stuff defines them, their possessions own them as opposed to them owning their possessions.

~MAJOR REGRET~ There are two regrets that I have in life. The first I am resolving this year, and it's that I have never traveled. Whether I have the money or not, I am going to travel this year. The second regret is that I have never had a long-term relationship. There are a lot of reasons for that, a combination of, I have never met the right person, but also, the past five years have been incredibly turbulent for me. Women aren't too crazy about guys who bet the house. I will resolve this regret as well.

~FAVOURITE QUOTE~ "To succeed in life, you need two things: ignorance and confidence" by Mark Twain inspired me a few years ago, and I modified it to "There are only two things you need for success: courage and ignorance." This modified quote has kept on coming back to me over the past couple of years, and it's pretty dead on.

~INFLUENTIAL BOOK~ *The Grapes of Wrath* by John Steinbeck had a profound impact on my life. Not only is it a beautifully, profoundly written book, the guy ended up winning a Nobel Prize, but it is also a book about social justice. It's a book about people, about the "haves" and the "have nots", and I have been an underdog all my life. I have been a "have not" all my life. Even when I was making the money that I was making while working in the corporate world, I always considered myself to be on the outside and a "have not".

The story takes place during the depression of the 1930s and it's about a family of subsistence farmers or sharecroppers in Oklahoma. Their son gets out of prison for murdering a guy, and they feel that they are going to lose the farm, be kicked off the farm by the corporation that owns it. They get a handbill, which said that they were looking for help in California, so they decide to all go to California because of the jobs there.

They leave their farm and travel to California to look for work. What they didn't realize was that there were cars traveling across the desert into California like ants. The problem was that everyone was getting the same handbill. As the book unfolds page after page, you sit there and think that no good can come from this, and you turn the page and you think again, no good can come from this. And, the family gets further and further into pure shit, and Steinbeck's brilliance as a writer, is that even though you think that no good can come from this, you are left with the feeling that the family can somehow survive because that's the kind of people they are, and because of the kind of people they come from. It's kind of written into the DNA code of people who survive. It's a brilliant, brilliant book. It's pure genius.

"There are only two things you need for success: courage and ignorance."

-Gabriel Draven (Inspired by Mark Twain's Quote)

95

 SUZANNE GIBSON
FUNDRAISING WITH A TWIST

"What stirs the mind or touches the heart, will undoubtedly move the feet." -Donald Murphy

~CHALLENGE~ In 1996, the Canadian Non-profit Housing Foundation approached me to conduct a feasibility study to figure out how a national organization could raise funds and support homelessness organizations locally across the country.

The business challenge was figuring out what was viable, and then implement. It was from the conception of idea, to putting a business plan together to implementation and evaluation. At the time, homelessness was not on the public agenda and most people were not even supporting the issue locally, so to look at it as a national fundraising and revenue generating initiative was in itself a challenge.

In addition, the Canadian Non-profit Housing Foundation didn't have a high profile and had virtually no money. By the time the feasibility study was done, the organization had about $15,000 to implement the idea. The organization didn't have a track record of programming, but it had an excellent board of directors of homelessness experts.

~RESOLUTION~ I believe in the power of best practices, so my colleague and I talked to over 30 experts across Canada who were well positioned to give us advice. After the consultations, we had a lot of really good strategic advice and feedback, however we didn't have a concept or idea. While we both had fundraising experience, there was nothing that was going to work, given the limited amount of money we had to invest. We needed a big idea that would take off. We looked at best practices in the United States and the United Kingdom, and focused on four organizations that had had really good success. We identified the factors and elements in each of those organizations that had contributed to its success, and picked out the ones that would fit best in the Canadian context, configured a strategy, a mission, an organization, and an action plan based on that.

We now had a feasibility study and a business plan. The business plan was a big thinking idea. It was about using comics, doing comedy events and promoting an icon (the Canadian toque). It had a lot of "pluckiness." With only $15,000, it was a really bold idea.

Our first job was to give the organization a name. Donald Murphy, an advertising genius came up with the name "Raising the Roof," an ideal name since it epitomized the idea of creating shelter and had a celebratory energy to it that captured our high-energy comedy approach.

Over three years, we took the $15,000 and generated $1.3 million. We also secured $1.4 million worth of value in media coverage in addition to building an infrastructure, revenue base, and volunteer base. We designed and launched a pilot, which we tested in Toronto. We proved that it worked then moved toward a scale up across the country. We expanded into the west (Vancouver) and east (Halifax) to gain a national presence.

In the second year, we secured Royal Bank as a significant national sponsor. They were involved in many layers of activities and they played a key role in our success.

We targeted other groups to negotiate what we could do for them and what they could do for us. Our strategy to align with as many groups as possible paid off. For us, marketing was the key element and we had to be very creative. We leveraged recognizable icons like the toque (that hat you put on your head to keep it warm) for "raising the roof." The toque is Canadian and makes you think of a roof over your head concept, which fit with our issue.

97

~LESSONS LEARNED~

1. Talk to experts, pick their brains, get different perspectives, and look at best practices

2. When doing something new, you have to test the concept before investing in a scale up

3. With little financial resources, we had to market and sell the concept to a few key investors who would stay with us over a minimum of three years and provide seed support

4. It's important to "cobble" together dedicated staff. We didn't have the money to pay the staff, but we all worked part-time. They were skilled, passionate and highly motivated. Nothing can be done without a team approach

5. It was critical to create an advisory group of supporters who were well positioned and influential to open doors for us

6. I learned the value of partnerships and connecting with already existing groups, and seeing our cause as a movement

continued on next page

7. I learned the hard way about balance between assessing what you can do with the resources that you have when you start something. I still struggle with how to start something with nothing and resource it effectively and humanely!

8. I learned about the challenges of managing diverse agendas. We had a lot of different stakeholders, including businesses, corporations, faith groups with different agendas. We had to remind ourselves of what our agenda was and carefully renegotiate to ensure we met our mission and desired outcomes

9. I assumed the role of Executive Director in a part-time capacity and worked on it for four years. By the time I was finished, I had built up the funding base and I had built up the staffing base and I built up everything that needed to be built up but there wasn't a succession plan per se. We had a hard time finding a new executive director

10. I learned about the power of people and how all these "angels" fell from the sky and participated in giving to the cause. Things only ever happen because many hands till the soil. Synergy is at the heart of all successful endeavours

~HOW TO INTEGRATE YOUR PERSONAL AND PROFESSIONAL LIFE~ This is about balance, and I struggle with it because my professional work is in the charity sector. The social justice side of it feeds my personal life and feeds my deep inner mission or longing that I have, to try and contribute to do something better. The balance between my personal and professional life can get blurred because I get over zealous at times and do a lot of volunteer work. To balance myself, I have a physical fitness training program, a meditation and spiritual practice. I get out in nature and try to keep the people in my life, who I love, close to me. If I feed myself personally I am much better professionally.

~FORMULA FOR SUCCESS~ The formula for success is about your leadership posture. If you are trying to start a business or trying to do something new you're innovating. When you innovate you are in a leadership role, and you have to involve others and give them ownership, and create what I call "roving" leadership, where you let people pick-up things and run with them. You need to inspire and cajole, get people involved, and be very open to learning, where you don't have the answers but you facilitate the answers. Your job is to keep your eye on the horizon and remind others what the point of what you're doing is. It's holding your vision and inspiring people toward the end goal, but weaving in their expertise, knowledge and skills, and do it with humility, grace and from a place of recognizing that there needs to be a multitude of people and voices or it won't take off.

To summarize, the formula for success is to create a learning organization, be open, take risks, think outside the box, be open to change, and know how to manage other people's expectations and help them see a new roadmap to get to the end, even though everything has changed. You also have to under-promise and over-deliver!

~**MAJOR REGRET**~ Things go wrong that I regret, but when I look back with perspective I do not ever regret anything. I realize that there is always something potent to take from the experience. I had a situation where a personal relationship fell apart and we both played into it. At the time it ate me up, I had regrets about my personal behaviour, but in the end, I look back and there were magnificent lessons to learn about myself and about how I live in the world and how I can be better, more compassionate, more connected when I relate to people. When I make business mistakes I see it as an opportunity to strengthen my muscles and become a better person by being more effective at what I do. You take what you get from something and I don't want to take regret.

99

~**FAVOURITE QUOTE**~ I go through phases where a quote affects me. Right now it's Donald Murphy's "What stirs the mind or touches the heart, will undoubtedly move the feet." I feel an affinity to the quote because I feel overwhelmed by all that's going on in the world, and I often wonder what can I do as one person. This quote tells me that if we can inspire others and feed their hearts and stimulate their minds we can motivate action for positive change.

~**INFLUENTIAL BOOK**~ A person made a difference in my life. When I was in my early twenties, Ratna Omidvar mentored me and took me under her wings when I was just starting in the field. She told me that I could accomplish anything I wanted, my heart's dream, because I was smart and talented. She let me know that she was there to help me develop my skills. In that early stage of my career, she catapulted my self-belief, catapulted me into positions and opportunities that I wouldn't have gotten elsewhere. She has dramatically changed my life in terms of my work, and my understanding of how to support other people. Because of being mentored by her, I now mentor others because I can see what a dramatic difference it can make in someone's life.

JANICE LAWRENCE-CLARKE
BRINGING A NEW PRODUCT TO THE RIGHT CLIENTS

"I can do all things through Him who strengthens me."
(Philippians 4:13, The New Testament)

~CHALLENGE~ I designed The Incubator 2005, a Sales and Marketing program for fashion and accessory designers who currently produce and sell to U.S. stores and were ready to take the next step toward a larger presence in the market. Through a combination of fashion consulting, market development, advertising and sales representation, these designers would be able to present their merchandise at trade events before retail buyers with purchasing power. I calculated the costs and determined that with a minimum of five participants the program could be properly implemented while being affordable for each company. The designers loved the program, but were not financially prepared to take that step. I realized that I was speaking or selling my service to the wrong market segment, so I had to clearly identify my market and repackage the program.

~RESOLUTION~ I reworked the entire program, creating three phases for a broader base appeal, thereby increasing the ability to address the designer/manufacturer at different levels in their businesses. Specifically, I had to:

1. Determine services for those designers who were relatively new to the market:

   a. Focus on building their collection
   b. Source production facilities
   c. Source manufacturing facilities
   d. Act as a broker to find investors who had facilities and sought fashion designers with a collection or line to produce

2. Provide public relations services for those designers who have been in business, but needed help in getting the word out about their company, or who may be wanting to present a line to the market

3. Secure showroom space to present collections to buyers during the selling season

I also developed strategic relationships with some specialty stores to test certain designers' collections.

~LESSONS LEARNED~

1. It is advantageous to line up the right product or service with the right market. Even though you may think that you have a brilliant idea or program, you need to do research to ensure that your product/idea is solid for the people to whom you're selling

2. Be prepared to accept that people may not be as ready as you are to move forward or to take leaps of faith

3. You must be willing to start from scratch and be willing to take less of a fee when introducing a new concept

4. It helped me to zero in on what my services are, and who my target market is. My success depends on the success of others. I learned to zero in and treat myself as one of my clients. (Sounds like the Business Plan, doesn't it?)

~HOW TO INTEGRATE YOUR PERSONAL AND PROFESSIONAL LIFE~ It's all about proper time management. We have one life and things constantly overlap. I am a mother, very active in my church, and some church members are my clients. My daughter is a teenager, and she helps me in my business whenever it is necessary. Above all I rely on the Holy Spirit for guidance, and have learned to say "No" when I have to do so. It's important to know when to say "No."

~FORMULA FOR SUCCESS~ It is best to be spirit-led. You find God's will for your life, and you perform that will. You allow Him, to work through you, knowing that once you are in His will, you can do all things through Christ who strengthens you. Never give up, no matter what it looks like, nor what the nay saying well-wishers may say. According to my pastor, Creflo Dollar, "Passion is the fuel of success …," that means to me, that I must be passionate about whatever I set about to do, do it as if I'm doing it for God and not for man, and I will succeed. And that message translates to any situation, whether it is self-employment or out in the work field or just being a friend… any and all areas of life. Above all, stay focused on God and do not listen to naysayers.

~MAJOR REGRET~ My major regret is allowing well-wishers to hold more sway over what I did and knew in my heart. Had I stuck to what I knew and believed, I would have been further ahead. Before these days, I did not have the wisdom or strength to realize that I was on my path and should have stayed focused.

~FAVOURITE QUOTE~ I like "I can do all things through Him who strengthens me" Philippians 4:13 because it is true! I'm a living witness. Now that I know this, there is nothing that anyone can tell me that I cannot do.

~INFLUENTIAL BOOK~ It has to be *The Successful Family: Everything You Need To Know To Build A Successful Family*, by Dr. Creflo A. Dollar and Taffi L. Dollar. This book, together with *The Holy Bible*, has opened my eyes and showed me how to live as a true Christian woman, as well as how to raise my child. It outlines practical ways to live a happy, healthy and prosperous life while building great relationships. It has had, and continues to have a great impact on my life.

JOSEPH MARTIN
A DIFFERENT KIND OF UNIVERSITY COURSE

"Those who cannot learn from history are doomed to repeat it."
George Santayana

~CHALLENGE~ The business challenge that I faced was raising the funds and gaining acceptance for a Canadian business history course at a Canadian business school. The University of Toronto requires $3 million funding for a chair. This was the easier of the two challenges. Getting acceptance was somewhat more difficult because the decision-making process at an academic institution is not always clear. In my 11 years at the University I have never been totally involved, which was an initial barrier.

~RESOLUTION~ Roger Martin, the Dean for the Rotman School of Business was extremely helpful, and Red Wilson, one of Canada's most prominent businessmen was instrumental in raising the necessary funds. We developed a fundraising plan, which included:

103

- 4 gifts of $250,000
- 2 gifts of $1 million

Red and Dick Currie each contributed $1 million. Hal Jackman and Tony Fell contributed $250,000 each. Jim Fleck also gave $250,000 and because he was a faculty member the University matched it. Finally, John McArthur, a Canadian and Dean Emeritus of Harvard Business School donated US $50,000 – this helped to add credibility to what we were trying to do.

I was able to overcome the challenges because there was growing interest in what I was trying to accomplish.

~LESSONS LEARNED~

1. I had to relearn the many levels of approval needed in an academic setting. The best way to describe it is that the "devil is in the details." For example, we commissioned 10 cases for the course. When we received the cases, a great deal of time was spent designing the cover for the cases, discussing copyright issues, deciding on contact details if more copies were needed. Small things cropped up that we didn't think of. These details took nearly as much time as developing the actual cases.

2. There are always policy decisions in an academic environment

3. We got the funding because the course was Canadian focused

~HOW TO INTEGRATE YOUR PERSONAL AND PROFESSIONAL LIFE~ My wife would say that I do not integrate my personal and professional life as well as I should, but I think that I have always done a reasonable job. We have four children and seven grandchildren. My children are very different. Politically, they are from one side of the spectrum to the other – conservative to green party. We are also very involved in our grandchildren's lives – we make time to watch their hockey games. I always make time for my family, and the trick is to do the unexpected and not just the expected.

~FORMULA FOR SUCCESS~ There is no magic to it! The formula for success is discipline and hard work. I keep a daily diary which I review every Sunday. During the review, I summarize how the week went and then I go back a year before to look at the lessons learned to determine how best to plan. I randomly look at past diaries to assess how I did and am doing. Every half decade I summarize. These actions help me to accomplish my goals and stay focused.

~MAJOR REGRET~ My biggest regret is my lack of formal education. I have an honours degree in history and an honorary doctorate. I wish that I had at least a Masters degree. While I was a partner at Deloitte and Touche the firm sent me to do the 13-week Advanced Management program at Harvard Business School, which I really appreciated.

~FAVOURITE QUOTE~ I like "Those who cannot learn from history are doomed to repeat it" by George Santayana and another quote by the businessman who said "the reason I study history is so that I can make my own mistakes" because I am trying to teach students that there is much knowledge in the world.

In addition, in the mid 1980s when I was at the top of my game, I knew exactly what I needed to do. I conducted some research and discovered a 10-year old report that contained a blueprint of what I was planning to implement. Why wasn't this blueprint implemented? Why did it fail? History allows you to evaluate and learn.

~INFLUENTIAL BOOK~ *Beyond Certainty: The Changing Worlds of Organizations* by Charles Handy had a profound impact on me. Handy explains that when you get to your mid 50s you shouldn't have a job, but a "portfolio life," which is a portfolio of things to do. Examples of Handy's "portfolio life" include the following:

1. Paid work: remunerated on a time basis

2. Contract work: remunerated according to the results obtained

3. Household work: carried out as part of managing and maintaining a household

4. Volunteer work: done for charity organizations, one's community, friends, family and neighbours

5. Educational work: carried out for purposes of learning, professional development, reading, increasing our level of culture

I decided to take early retirement from being a partner at the consulting firm where I had worked for years. I took Charles Handy's advice and created my portfolio of things to do.

1. Get an academic position

2. Be a corporate director

3. Continue to consult as a sole practitioner

4. Focus on history

5. Focus on Family

Over a decade later I am doing what I set out to do in my portfolio. I have now realized that there is too much in my portfolio and trying to focus more.

> *"The reason I study history is so that I can make my own mistakes."* -Businessman

ANTHEA ROSSOUW
LEADING WOMEN TOWARD SELF-SUFFICIENCY

"We are all caught in an inescapable network of mutuality, tied into a single garment of destiny, whatever affects one directly, affect all indirectly." Martin Luther King (Letter from Birmingham Jail)

~CHALLENGE~ Starting Dreamcatcher was a challenge of itself, considering that everything that I do is centred on something that has never been done before in South Africa. I harnessed the women in disadvantaged communities across South Africa in an effort to put "an end to aid without end," to put an end to poverty, and bring long-term solutions to their own future. Convincing these women - who had no confidence in themselves to run their own business - to identify with the project, and develop their own micro businesses, using available resources, was a challenge.

In South Africa, those who controlled and ran businesses in the travel and tourism industry before the end of apartheid are still reaping the lion's share of the income generated from the industry. Ninety-nine percent of these people are those who never had contact with the culture on a social or business level. Therefore, the women along with their cultures in their communities across South Africa are strangers to them. Culture was not sold as an important tourism product, and the animals and safaris were always over-emphasized. So, people who were not into the animal-safari sector did not understand that the people living among these animals were the custodians of these environments.

People then, and today, are sceptical and do not see the significance of involving the local communities as BUSINESSMEN & WOMEN in their own right. These BUSINESSMEN & WOMEN hold the key to a long-term plan for saving tourism in South Africa generating an income through enterprises because they understand the importance of the women in their communities.

Another major challenge was expanding tourism in all regions, as well as developing the businesses surrounding tourism. This meant enhancing the tourism experience in South Africa with authentic cultural contact in community accommodation, cuisine, and craft, which would benefit the women in the communities and foster their children's development.

~RESOLUTION~ I overcame the major challenge by taking the authentic cultural experiences, and the women entrepreneurs who would benefit directly from it, into the marketplace to create awareness in the tourist market. I developed very basic human interactive tourism and travel experiences to rebuild communities, pride and the local economy. For each $100 a micro entrepreneur earns, the return is five-fold. When you are poor you do not need bags of money to sustain yourself. It's when you are rich that you do!

A challenge is only a challenge when you do not see an end with an outcome. If I had been intimidated by the challenge, Dreamcatcher would not have materialized. In a challenge, you look for the opportunities. The thought of NOT doing this does not cross my mind. There is no other alternative to long-term poverty alleviation in the communities across South Africa and in Southern Africa.

~LESSONS LEARNED~

1. Do not rely on politicians to effect change when it comes to economic empowerment. Political liberation never ensures economic liberation from poverty

2. Don't take no for an answer and be passionate about making a difference

3. You have to look for like-minded people, create a network, and then you can make a difference and make it work together in a strategic partnership

4. Travel and tourism can be the biggest liberator of poverty because it's the world's biggest industry, and it's completely people-based. If you can get to the people who spend their money on travel, you can direct them to spend their money where it will make a difference

5. Do not accept the way things have been done. Travel and tourism have been controlled by "mass" and "bus window" tourism experiences, and that's the way most mainstream travel agencies are run. They are not interested in spreading the benefits at grassroots

6. It will help us little in Africa to try to save the environment, the rhinos and the elephants, if people who are the custodians, do not benefit from these actions. Destitute people do not understand the need to preserve the forest if they are hungry, or they look the other way when they are enticed to poach, or become involved in clandestine activities when offered money

7. To build a better Africa and world, we should not alienate the local people, or prevent them from interacting with tourists. World peace and harmonious coexistence is directly linked to the attitudes of people. We cannot talk of being safe in our homes from an elevated comfort zone, or being safe during our holiday, or in our business, when we ignore the impact of tourism on people

~HOW TO INTEGRATE YOUR PERSONAL AND PROFESSIONAL LIFE~ I believe in any human interaction that will create a better world. The human contact with my family and the quality time that I spend with them is the same as the quality time that I spend with the many women I work with. I am not a different person when I am with family than when I am with others. There is no difference between the two. I'm not two people. It's too difficult to be that way! My family supports everything that I do and I support them. I make time for introspection with my family and when I do so, I like to retreat into nature. Peace descends on me when I am outside in nature, and the environment gives me strength. It gives me the strength and energy to interact with people on both the personal and professional level. When I watch the trees and hear the breeze, I know that there is a bigger purpose.

~FORMULA FOR SUCCESS~ Commitment! You have to believe in what you are doing and be committed to it, because your desires lead to deeds, which lead to your destiny.

~MAJOR REGRET~ I should have started 20 years ago spreading my message of hope and the alleviation of poverty, instead of waiting for people with vested interests in the status quo to help me get the message out. Only when I realized that I had to take my message directly to the people outside South Africa did I see that an end is possible.

A defining moment for me was when I was almost a victim of 9/11. I changed my flight from the one that went into the north tower a few days before the tragedy. I was scheduled to give a talk to a group in California when I realized that my time with them would be too short so I changed my flight and flew to Dallas. That decision changed my life. I spent six days travelling on trains and buses all over the United States trying to get back to South Africa. During that time, seeing people in their darkest moments of fear, I realized that the fear was not only a fear of terrorists, but also lack of knowledge of other cultures and about each other. I realized that my purpose was written all over the fear and heartache I experienced in America. I had a mission to build peace through human contact for cultural harmony. That was the moment, all alone with no food on a train full of fearful people that I made the decision to reach out with our Kamammas (community matriarchs). I was now going to take this message of hope to empower the women with micro businesses, foster micro businesses between cultures and share my passion for a better life for the many poor women and their destitute children whom I have met in all the years of Apartheid.

~FAVOURITE QUOTE~ I like "We are all caught in an inescapable network of mutuality, tied into a single garment of destiny, whatever affects one directly, affect all indirectly" by Martin Luther King (Inspired by Ghandi) and "We are made to live together because of the interrelated structure of reality" by Martin Luther King because I identify with them and they relate to life's realities. "If we don't learn from history we will repeat it," my incredible mother always said. What happens in one country, impacts other countries. We are bound by mutual destiny. I can make a difference by becoming involved in the destiny of the world. You work locally but think globally.

~INFLUENTIAL BOOK~ Two books have made a major difference to my life: *I Know Why the Caged Bird Sings* and *All God's Children Need Traveling Shoes* both by Maya Angelou. In *I Know Why the Caged Bird Sings*, the central message for my situation is, that if women are caged in by poverty and all the terrible social evils in their community, do they shrivel up and die because of these given circumstances? Or, do they use their hospitality and their humanity and their skills to welcome, to reach out and to be heard outside? And in so doing create their own destiny and a better life. Poor Mr. Nelson Mandela – he is still seeing so much of a "bitter life" instead of the "better life" he dreamed about for our country. It is a great feeling to know that this incredible patriarch needs me to bring that dream to fruition, just as my children and I needed him to fight for the end of Apartheid. Do you see the mutuality? We need to bring people into South Africa to share our rich culture. A woman can make a difference even if she finds herself caged in her poor community. She has herself. No one can take that from her – only herself.

In the case of *All God's Children Need Traveling Shoes*, only when people travel to South Africa and see how they can reach out via their travels, can we make a difference. We need to take the Kamammas, and help them to don their travelling shoes, so that they can tell their stories and "put an end to aid without end".

> *"We are made to live together because of the interrelated structure of reality."* Martin Luther King

110

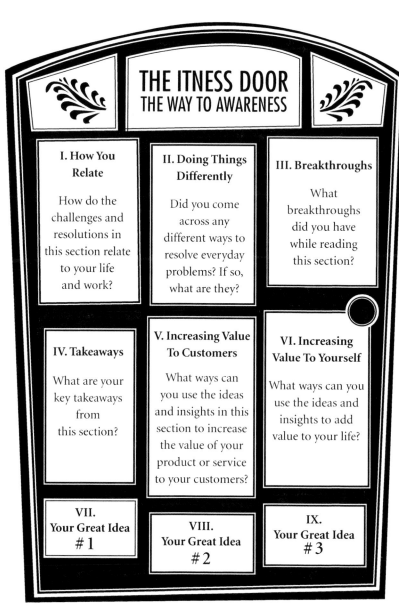

THE ITNESS DOOR
THE WAY TO AWARENESS

I. How You Relate

How do the challenges and resolutions in this section relate to your life and work?

II. Doing Things Differently

Did you come across any different ways to resolve everyday problems? If so, what are they?

III. Breakthroughs

What breakthroughs did you have while reading this section?

IV. Takeaways

What are your key takeaways from this section?

V. Increasing Value To Customers

What ways can you use the ideas and insights in this section to increase the value of your product or service to your customers?

VI. Increasing Value To Yourself

What ways can you use the ideas and insights to add value to your life?

VII. Your Great Idea #1

VIII. Your Great Idea #2

IX. Your Great Idea #3

111

112

UNIVERSAL LESSONS LEARNED

1. *Look for like-minded people, create a network and then you can make a difference and make it work together in strategic partnership*
   ~Anthea Rossouw

2. *Do not take no for an answer. Do not accept the way things have been done. Be passionate about making a difference in a tangible way*
   ~Anthea Rossouw

3. *Do not alienate the local people, or prevent them from interacting with tourists. World peace and harmonious coexistence are directly linked to the attitudes of people*
   ~Anthea Rossouw

4. *Follow the golden rule: Do unto other as you would have them do unto you*
   ~Lydia Danner

5. *When you're starting off, it takes ten times more energy than you thought*
   ~Maria Nemeth

6. *Even though you have a goal of where you want to go, you have to realize that you may have to alter it in some way as you go. Try to be as clear as you can about which things are important to hold firm to and which to let go*
   ~Ann Kirkland

7. *Recognize the divergence between what you as a professional view as your ethical standard, and what some clients see as merely a stance that is variable on request*
   ~Oliver Campbell

8. *Find out which issues are impacting people's decision-making then address them*
   ~Arunas Chesonis

9. *Staff will always leave but that doesn't mean that you shouldn't invest in training for them*
   ~Asha McLeod

10. *In a strategic partnership, make sure that you are both flexible, and that the business relationship is advantageous to both parties, consider each other's interest*
    ~Chris Widener

113

11. *When things appear bleak, you can throw up your hands and jump off a tall building or deal with the situation*
~Claire Hoy

12. *If you nurture and care for your staff, you'll reap the benefits*
~Samy Chong

13. *Problems are often complex and you need to find a multifaceted solution*
~Stephen Abram

14. *There is no way that you can do everything so don't go it alone*
~Gail Blanke

15. *Cultures are different and there are no cookbook solutions for working together in groups. People are individually very different, and to be a good leader you must spend time observing and talking to those you work with*
~Simon Grant

114

SECTION 2
PART 4: PERSONAL BELIEF SYSTEM

OLIVER CAMPBELL

LEA CHAMBERS

LYDIA DANNER

MARIA NEMETH

OLIVER CAMPBELL
PROFESSIONAL RISKS

"For what are your possessions but things you keep and guard for fear you might need them tomorrow? And tomorrow, what shall tomorrow bring to the over-prudent dog burying bones in the trackless sand as he follows the pilgrims to the holy city?"

-Kahlil Gibran

~CHALLENGE~ The main business challenge an accountant in public practice faces, arises as a matter of professional risk. One client asked me to prepare two sets of books, one for normal reporting and another for the tax authorities.

~RESOLUTION~ I refused to do so, pointing out the drawbacks of preparing varying records, in addition to the illegality of the request. I ceased doing business with that client.

116

~LESSONS LEARNED~

1. The main lesson relates to recognizing the divergence between what I as a professional view as my ethical standard, and what some clients see as merely a stance that is variable on request

2. The loss of a client is not necessarily a negative. New business opportunities constantly arise and the loss of a client may in fact allow you to accept new business

~HOW TO INTEGRATE YOUR PERSONAL AND PROFESSIONAL LIFE~ I like to think that my personal and professional lives are separate. I try not to accept any position in my personal social life, which requires me to use my accounting skills or to control financial resources.

Despite this, it is never easy to accomplish a total separation. The personal values, which are used in your business life are also those which guide your social activities. Among other things, I teach Sunday School, and the same clarity which I attempt to achieve in accounting and financial reporting is the same clarity which I attempt to impart when I am advising my students on how their belief system should guide their actions in daily living.

~FORMULA FOR SUCCESS~ I do not think there is a formula, which will ensure success. Each person will find that success arrives in different ways. Success is not always measurable in monetary terms, though this is the most frequently used measure. There are countless persons who were successful in their chosen field of activity who did not enjoy monetary success.

There are factors, which seem to lead to success. One factor is the striving for excellence. Many persons who set out to give of their best find that recognition and monetary reward follows. Another factor is family. Many persons who are successful give great credit to the support of their families. Certainly financial success, which persists, seems to run in families and the support system created by genealogical affiliation.

~MAJOR REGRET~ My regret lies in my education and socialization. These were geared to prepare me to attain and retain employment, rather than to encourage me to take entrepreneurial action.

~FAVOURITE QUOTE~ I like "For what are your possessions but things you keep and guard for fear you might need them tomorrow? And tomorrow, what shall tomorrow bring to the over-prudent dog burying bones in the trackless sand as he follows the pilgrims to the holy city?" by Kahlil Gibran because it indicates that life is an endless progression of change. To be overly careful by repeating actions, which may appear to be wise can become very foolish if we do not recognize the nature of the progressions facing us.

117

~INFLUENTIAL BOOK~ *The Prophet* by Kahlil Gibran was particularly influential in my decision to leave Jamaica and complete my professional exams in the United Kingdom. The author was a very spiritual person who was also blessed with genius. I define genius as someone who has the ability to make complex things simple. Genius resides not only in persons of great intellect, but also in persons with outstanding physical and athletic ability. The genius of Gibran is shown in the simplicity of his writings, which at the same time set out the most profound observations about the human condition.

LEA CHAMBERS
OFFICE POLITICS

"Our deepest fear is not that we are inadequate. Our deepest fear is that we are powerful beyond measure. It is our light, not our darkness that most frightens us. We ask ourselves, "Who am I to be brilliant, gorgeous, talented, fabulous?" Actually, who are you not to be? You are a child of God..."

–Marianne Williamson

~**CHALLENGE**~ The most memorable business challenge of my career thus far revolves around the challenges in internal politics in the workplace.

A few years ago, I was the lead on an extremely large national ad/marketing campaign at a significantly sized Canadian financial services company. The campaign was being driven by the Senior VP of our Marketing Department, who decided that our fall campaign (also run by myself) had not been effective enough and the company needed a campaign that was more fresh and ambitious than the award winning campaign we had just finished working on. Our entire team was exhausted from the previous effort, but he asked us to pull off one more effort, and decided that a smaller program that had been created by myself was ready to be taken to the "next level" in terms of its exposure to our client base.

I was devastated by all this. Not only was I exhausted from having executed a full campaign already that quarter, but the program he had decided to "champion" was my baby, a really intelligent concept that I had nurtured and grown slowly over time and was growing at the ground level with our sales force and some select clients. He proposed to change it all - change the main concepts, change the design, change how it was presented, and he asked me to do all the changing. I knew the market wasn't ready for it and told him this, but to no avail.

~**RESOLUTION**~ I executed a $1 million national ad/media/website/collateral/sales training campaign in two months and burnt myself out in the process. Did I have a choice? I suppose, but saying "no" wasn't really an option. It broke my heart to change all of the materials I had taken so much time to write. I spent long days at the office pulling it all off and put on a happy face "for the team", but wasn't truly happy about it all. But I did it anyway and left the company shortly after.

118

~LESSONS LEARNED~

1. I learned that we don't "own" anything we build for large corporations, so I learned to detach myself from my work

2. I learned how far I can push myself to get a project done, and how large the cost is of doing that

3. And, in the end, I learned to walk away. I learned the boundaries of how I'll be treated by a company. Similar things had happened to colleagues who are still there. I made the choice to take a stand and leave an environment that was not respectful of the great efforts of good people. It was the best thing that has happened to me so far in my career

~HOW TO INTEGRATE YOUR PERSONAL AND PROFESSIONAL LIFE ~I think one's attitude about what exactly their "job" is influences how they integrate their personal and professional life. Our real "JOB" in life has nothing to do with our "job". Our "JOB" in life is to awaken to who we truly are - to experience the greatest level of freedom and achievement we can in all aspects of our lives and to BE who we are as fully as we can in each moment. In this perspective, there is no separation between personal and professional life. We just ARE, in each moment and seek fulfillment in each moment regardless of the situation. If we ARE, our "job" will simply be a reflection of who we are inside. Our "job" will be in alignment with our belief systems, our passions and our inner unfolding.

119

~FORMULA FOR SUCCESS~ Success is the awareness in each moment of who you ARE and the celebration of your Unfolding as you go through your Life, regardless of changing circumstances. Having this perspective allows you to adapt to change and any situation. When you are focusing on BEING, you simply allow your Life to unfold right in front of you in a detached sort of way. And, funnily enough, you begin to experience more abundance in all aspects of your life than you ever imagined possible.

~MAJOR REGRET~I believe we only regret the things in life we DON'T do, not the things we do. So my regrets so far, at the age of 35? Hmmm... I'm not really sure I have any. I've done everything I've wanted to do at this stage of my life and have lots of adventures ahead. I've loved everyone in

my life as much as I could, given where I was at and have done my best to be kind to as many people as possible.

~FAVOURITE QUOTE~ Our Deepest Fear

Our deepest fear is not that we are inadequate, our deepest fear is that we are powerful beyond measure.

It is our light, not our darkness, that most frightens us.

We ask ourselves,

"Who am I to be brilliant, gorgeous, talented and fabulous?"

Actually, who are you not to be?

You are a child of God.

Your playing small does not serve the world.

There is nothing enlightening about shrinking so that other people won't feel insecure around you.

We were born to manifest the glory that is within us.

And as we let our light shine, we unconsciously give other people permission to do the same.

As we are liberated from our own fear, our presence automatically liberates others.

Marianne Williamson, *A Return To Love: Reflections on the Principles of A Course in Miracles*, Harper Collins, 1992. From Chapter 7, Section 3

I like this quote because it reminds me not to be less than I am so that others can feel better about themselves. I often receive feedback from others that they feel inadequate around me... And it encourages me to always BE and shine the Light that is inside of me.

~INFLUENTIAL BOOK~ Definitely *The Prophet* by Kahlil Gibran. I read
it when I was 17 years old and it has always served as a source of inspiration and wisdom, especially in times (and years) when life was really challenging.

Kahlil Gibran was a Persian spiritual leader and poet prevalent in the early 20th century. His book, *The Prophet* is a series of poems containing wisdom about all aspects of life and the challenges we face as we go "home."

LYDIA DANNER
LISTEN, HEAR, GIVE

"Be the change you want to see in the world." -Mahatma Gandhi

~CHALLENGE~ As a fringe dweller, I have not had business challenges in the traditional sense. I have always worked alone. Having said that, I have had many satisfied clients. I LISTEN to what people need and GIVE it to them. If you LISTEN, people will tell you everything. Personally and Professionally. We are all family, after all. We are all one. We are all the same.

When the children were small, we had the same nanny for 13 happy years. Many people have asked me, "how did you keep the same nanny for all those years?" I LISTENED. And I gave her what she needed. What did she want? She wanted a family of her own. So I gave her mine. She wanted to be master of her own house. So I let her be master of mine. I had minimal guidelines (clean nurtured children, clean house and clean laundry). But she got to decide when and how those things were accomplished. I never interfered or imposed my own schedule on hers. The result, the children had a second mom they really loved and still do to this day, and I had PEACE OF MIND, and a clean house and great meals, and a friend that I will always love and cherish.

121

I do not make a distinction between one's personal life and one's business life. To me it is all ONE life, and if you are true to yourself, you should be the same person, personally and professionally. However, if pressed, I would have to say my idea of the most effective business model would be to not treat your employees as employees. Rather, treat them as you would treat yourself. Listen to what they want for themselves, and find a way to give it to them. You will be amazed at the result. The same goes for customers. Listen to what they want, and give it to them. It's simple, really.

Another important insight I have had is this: If you want things to change, change yourself.

I had a tumultuous relationship with my stepdaughter Kathy throughout her teenage years. I was young and inexperienced, and neither of us would give the other a break. It was spirit torturing! Then I had an epiphany, thanks to a course I took with Anthony Robbins involving walking on hot coals. (I have nothing but good to say about this man!)

~RESOLUTION~ If I wanted my relationship with Kathy to change, I must change. So I did. I decided to look at her with new eyes. It was amazingly simple. And as a result of me changing, she changed, slowly at first, but it was a beautiful experience. I changed from "wicked stepmother" to "wonderful stepmother." We are still very much in each other's lives, despite a divorce from her father in 1995. We love each other and I am eternally grateful to have her in my life. The same goes for her brother Paul, with whom I had a similar tumultuous relationship and now am grandmother to his three beautiful children.

If you are having a challenge on a business level, do not look at how to change others, or even how to change the situation. Look at a way to change yourself.

~LESSONS LEARNED~

1. What lessons did I learn from these two examples? Life is simple really. Follow the golden rule. Do unto others as you would have them do unto you.

122

~HOW TO INTEGRATE YOUR PERSONAL AND PROFESSIONAL LIFE~ I do not draw a distinction between the two. To me, it is all LIFE. If you are true to yourself, it is easy to be true to others - friends, family and colleagues alike. Just be as authentically YOU as you can be in all situations.

~FORMULA FOR SUCCESS~ Do unto others as you would have them do unto you. And if you want things to change, change yourself, or change how you look at things.

~MAJOR REGRET~ I have NO regrets...not a single one. Everything that has happened to me, every decision that I have made, has led me to where I am now...I wouldn't want it any other way. Regret is a needless disrespect of God's plan.

~FAVOURITE QUOTE~ I like "Be the change you want to see in the world" by Gandhi and Namaste, loosely translated, it means, "The God in me recognizes (or sees) the God in you." It is easy and quite fashionable now to be in judgment and to criticize. People do it unconsciously, and they do not realize that their judgment and criticism CONTRIBUTE to the problem they are judging and criticizing. Not to mention that these acts also harm one's own spirit. If you take the work of Dr. Masuru Emoto, a Japanese researcher, and his study of water, when hateful things are directed toward water, it reacts by mutating its form. When loving things are directed, water reacts by forming beautiful, perfect crystals. Humans are about two-thirds water. When you direct a hateful thought or negative thought toward another human being, you are affecting their physiology. But equally horrifically, you are affecting YOUR OWN. Just think about it. Where does disease come from?

So, be the change you want to see in the world!

~INFLUENTIAL BOOK~ There is a saying: "When the student is ready the teacher will appear." Being a fringe dweller, my teachers have always come in the form of books. When my second parent died when I was six years old, a kind relative gave me *The Way to Heaven*. It's in German, but I still have it. When I was a teenager, I sought solace in the words of Leonard Cohen, and admire the man to this day. As an adult, when I quested for a spiritual centre, I started that quest with *Seth Speaks: The Eternal Validity of the Soul*. Other notable teachers are: *Excuse Me, Your Life is Waiting,* by Lynne Grabhorn; the whole *Conversations With God* series, written by Neale Donald Walsch; *In Resonance* and *Living on Light,* written by Jasmuheen; *Love Without End, Jesus Speaks* written by Glenda Green; and the *I AM Discourses*, Saint Germain Series "Volume 3," and *Ascended Master Instruction*, Saint Germain Series Volume 4; written by Saint Germain and other Ascended Masters.

123

Probably my favourite is: *The Little Soul and the Sun* by Neale Donald Walsh. It is a children's book, but I believe its message is ageless. I love it so much I always tell the story to others. I also recount it to all of the students in the classes that I teach.

It's a delightful story about a little perfect soul who wants God to grant him the experience of 'forgiveness'. God's explanation of what that would be like is really an explanation of what life is all about and why we are really here. It has had a profound influence on my life because its message resonates with my core spirit. It is in God's words. **"I have sent you nothing but Angels".**

Every time I encounter a person who has a challenge or is a challenge, or a situation that is a challenge, I remember that he/she is an angel, sent to me by God, so that I can raise myself to the highest level possible for me in this particular situation. The negative behaviours of others help me see what NOT to do, and how to rise above it. Negative situations are a gift. Negative people are a gift.

**All of Life is a gift. In reality, there are NO negatives, only gifts.
It's all good. And it's all so beautiful!**

"Namaste"

MARIA NEMETH
HOW TO SUCCEED WHEN YOU'RE NOT KNOWN

"Miracles rest not so much upon healing power coming suddenly near us from afar, but upon our perceptions being made finer, so that for the moment our eyes can see and our ears can hear what has been there around us always." -Willa Cather

~CHALLENGE~ In the beginning, I tried to get a seminar business off the ground and grow it at a time when nobody knew who I was. I encountered barriers. I learned that just because these obstacles were there, it didn't mean that my business was a bad idea. Everyone has to go through an initial stage of business development where things don't go smoothly.

~RESOLUTION~ I was persistent and did whatever it took to get the business idea into the physical reality, and ignored the "little voice" of doubt. I enlisted trusted friends as a support system, and made and kept promises such as making a few sales calls each day and educating people about what I had to offer. I took it one step at a time. I now operate a very successful seminar business, and it started with taking those small steps.

124

~LESSONS LEARNED~

1. Make and keep small promises. It could be a promise to make two sales calls a day because two are better than none. Each one takes you closer to your goals

2. When you're starting off, it takes ten times more energy than you thought necessary to grow a new business

3. You need a support structure in place to check in with you, encourage you and give you the courage to go on

~HOW TO INTEGRATE YOUR PERSONAL AND PROFESSIONAL LIFE~ I do not make a distinction. I do not have a personal or professional persona. Making a distinction makes your life more difficult. I try to show up as the same person wherever I am. It's more fun that way.

~FORMULA FOR SUCCESS~ The definition for success that we use at the Academy is to do what you say you're going to do in life, and do it with clarity, focus, ease and grace. That means your action is clear, you are focusing your energy, you're not struggling, and you're in touch with gratitude for simply being on this journey and having the capacity to achieve your goals and dreams in life.

~MAJOR REGRET~ I think I suffer from a regret that many of us have, which is that I didn't learn spiritual principles sooner rather than later. Once you finally see principles that work in your life, the first thing that happens is that you fall into the regret: "Why did it take me so long to wake up?" I have talked to so many people about this and they have this same regret for themselves. I think it's a part of the human condition to have that sense of regret.

~FAVOURITE QUOTE~ I like "Miracles rest not so much upon healing power coming suddenly near us from afar, but upon our perceptions being made finer, so that for the moment our eyes can see and our ears can hear what has been there around us always" by Willa Cather, a great American author. It's a wonderful quote about miracles. People think that miracles are things that happen to us suddenly from on high. I like this quote because it's hopeful, it says that I do not have to do anything extraordinary. All I need to do is wake up and see what's been here waiting for me all the time. It's already here and all is well. I think that everyone is looking for that sense that all is well.

125

~INFLUENTIAL BOOK~ The book that had a profound impact on my life is the *Autobiography of a Yogi* by Paramahansa Yogananda. This book is not only about Paramahansa Yogananda's life, but also about the lives of all the spiritually developed people that he met in India and Europe. The book is also about his philosophy, which combines the teachings of the Bhagavad-Gita with Christianity. It was his personal mission to bring what he calls the best of the west and the east together. It's a book that had a profound influence on a number of people's lives. For me, it was a book of such hope and sweetness. No matter what your religious orientation it spoke to the fact that we are all children of spirit, and the best thing for us to do is wake up and see this in our self and in others. This is why the *Autobiography of a Yogi* inspired me.

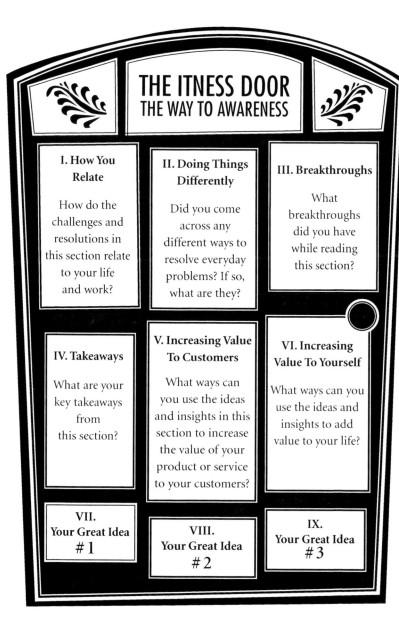

THE ITNESS DOOR
THE WAY TO AWARENESS

I. How You Relate

How do the challenges and resolutions in this section relate to your life and work?

II. Doing Things Differently

Did you come across any different ways to resolve everyday problems? If so, what are they?

III. Breakthroughs

What breakthroughs did you have while reading this section?

IV. Takeaways

What are your key takeaways from this section?

V. Increasing Value To Customers

What ways can you use the ideas and insights in this section to increase the value of your product or service to your customers?

VI. Increasing Value To Yourself

What ways can you use the ideas and insights to add value to your life?

VII. Your Great Idea #1

VIII. Your Great Idea #2

IX. Your Great Idea #3

126

127

128

NOTABLES

The Holy Bible got mentioned four times as an influential book

The Prophet by Kahlil Gibran got mentioned three times as an influential book

Autobiography of a Yogi by Paramhansa Yogananda got mentioned two times as an influential book

Lord of the Rings & *The Prophet* are two books that influenced people when they were teenagers

History got mentioned three times as an area of interest to study

The poem, "Our Deepest Fear" by Marianne Williamson was mentioned twice as a favourite quotation

Two of John C. Maxwell's books, *Winning With People* and *Your Roadmap For Success* influenced two people

Two of Maya Angelou's books, *All God's Children Need Traveling Shoes* and *I Know Why The Caged Bird Sings* influenced one person

Two people mentioned the importance of taking sabbaticals

Two people used handcuffs as a metaphor for preventing you from doing something – "bronze handcuff" and "handcuffed us in doing business"

Anthony Robbins got mentioned twice in reference to his courses

One person was influenced by the play, *Our Town* when she was 10 years old

129

130

SECTION 2
PART 5: TRUSTING/GETTING WHAT YOU NEED

MARY ELLEN BATES

GAIL BLANKE

GEORGE FRASER

ANDREA NIERENBERG

HEATHER RESNICK

CHRIS WIDENER

MARY ELLEN BATES
BALANCING MULTIPLE PRIORITIES

"Walking toward the fear is always a good idea. You're bigger than it is; you just don't know it yet" Jon Carroll

~CHALLENGE~ I'm one of those people who really do believe that challenges are opportunities that we haven't recognized yet. One challenge, which I've experienced twice now, is how to balance my various priorities while serving as president of the Association of Independent Information Professionals (AIIP). Being AIIP president means being on call for association and member crises at least five days a week, helping the AIIP directors lead their committees, stay focused on the long range goals of the association, attending to individual problems members are having with AIIP, and so on. I really value AIIP, so I took all these responsibilities very seriously. But, of course, without good time management skills, these could easily overwhelm the time and – even more importantly – the energy I have for my business and for the rest of my life.

~RESOLUTION~ Commit to spending the first hour of my day on AIIP matters, and then to focus on my business for the rest of the day. My greatest time/energy-management trick has been to shut down my email software for 4 or 5 hours at a time. Just knowing I can't ping my email every half hour helps me keep from getting distracted by dealing with immediate but not necessarily important issues.

~LESSONS LEARNED~

1. We info-entrepreneurs have to carefully manage our time, energy and concentration, since most of us are one-person businesses and if we're having a down day, the business has a down day

2. It's a matter of prioritizing, and examining each thing that demands our attention and deciding how essential it is

~HOW TO INTEGRATE YOUR PERSONAL AND PROFESSIONAL LIFE~ Well, having a home-based office helps a lot. I can take time off at noon to meet a friend, or leave work early to take the dogs on a hike. (Of course, I wind up paying for that by working longer hours the next day or on

132

the weekend, but that's an acceptable trade-off to me). And I have been able to build my business around my strengths and interests, and to structure my work so that the things I'm not as strong at aren't as needed.

~**FORMULA FOR SUCCESS**~ Do what you love, be prepared to do things you don't particularly enjoy doing to build and sustain your business, surround yourself with the things that revive your soul, don't take yourself too seriously, and give back to the profession – my most rewarding work is the volunteer work I do for AIIP.

~**MAJOR REGRET**~ None that I wish to share publicly.

~**FAVOURITE QUOTE**~ I like "Walking toward the fear is always a good idea. You're bigger than it is; you don't know it yet" by Jon Carroll, columnist for San Francisco chronicle (http://snipurl.com/fsbm) because it reminds me that things that are scary are do-able.

~**INFLUENTIAL BOOK**~ While I read compulsively, most books I read don't qualify as "life-changing". My life has been changed by the people I have in my life. As I said in the acknowledgements of my book, *Building and Running a Successful Research Business*, "I owe a special debt, which I'll never be able to repay, to Scott Smith, a dear friend and extraordinary person who, in the year I knew him before his death, taught me so much about living mindfully and listening carefully."

133

GAIL BLANKE
YOU DON'T HAVE TO GO IT ALONE

"There is no way it is, there is only the way you say it is. The universe hasn't made up its mind about you. It only knows what you show it today. You are the Inventor; your life is the invention. You get to make it up, so make it up good."
-Gail Blanke

~CHALLENGE~ After leaving the corporate world and becoming an entrepreneur, I believed that I had to do everything myself. I had a hard time trusting people; trusting that they would understand my vision and work as hard as I did.

I realized later that there were some good people to whom I didn't give a chance because I was afraid to trust them with my "baby." I kept everything very close to the chest, which isn't the way to expand and grow.

~RESOLUTION~ I finally realized that I couldn't do everything by myself and I now have a great partner who is involved in almost all aspects of my business.

~LESSONS LEARNED~

1. There is no way that you can do everything by yourself; don't go it alone

2. Trust, and anticipate that other people will be as committed as you are

3. Identify your "catcher," the person who backs you up, and "let the catcher do the catching"

~HOW TO INTEGRATE YOUR PERSONAL AND PROFESSIONAL LIFE~ Work/Life balance is a myth. Work and life are completely integrated. I have had an interesting career and worked throughout both my pregnancies. I went back to work six weeks after the first one and three months after the second.

I have a very close family and I constantly ask myself what am I committed to at this particular moment? At one instant, it might be attending a hockey game and at another it's working on a presentation. There were times when I opted out of a business trip because, in the end, my family always came first.

We have to learn to be easier on ourselves. We don't have to be everybody's everything all the time.

~FORMULA FOR SUCCESS~ Create a powerful vision of what you think your career or business should look like to propel you forward. Walt Disney said, "Build the castles first," because that's where the magic is. Always ask the all-important question: "How good could we make it?"

~FAVOURITE QUOTE~ My favourite quote is from my book, *Between Trapezes*, "There is no way it is, there is only the way you say it is. The universe hasn't made up its mind about you. It only knows what you show it today. You are the Inventor; your life is the invention. You get to make it up, so make it up good." This is my favourite quote because I'm passionate about persuading people that they get to decide how good their life will be!

~MAJOR REGRET~ I wish that I had been bolder. People who really succeed put their egos on the line and become unstoppable. The only thing standing between us and the world's most successful people is our willingness to hang in, keep going and insist on reaching our goal, our "Castle."

135

~INFLUENTIAL BOOK~ It wasn't a book but the play *Our Town* by Thornton Wilder. I saw this play when I was 10 years old and I have never forgotten it because it had such a profound impact on me. After I saw it, I made a promise to always let people know how much I love them, and I have kept that promise to this day.

Set at the turn of the 20th century, in the small town of Grover's Corners, New Hampshire, U.S.A., the play reveals the ordinary lives of the people, the tale of love, marriage and death and daily life. The play is centered on a woman, Emily, who dies during childbirth and wants to go back. Those who died before her allow her to go back for a day. Emily chooses to go back on her twelfth birthday. On her twelfth birthday she sees her family and suddenly realizes how much she took things for granted. She didn't appreciate how wonderful she had it at the time. Emily realizes how precious life is.

This play is about seizing the moment and living life fully in the moment. At 10 years old I made the promise, which I have kept, to let those near and dear to me know how much I love and appreciate them.

 **GEORGE FRASER**
PAY YOUR TAXES

First things first, second things never" -George Fraser

~CHALLENGE~ We did not pay our taxes in a timely manner and the federal government put a lien on all our funds. It handcuffed us in doing business.

~RESOLUTION~ We made a deal with the federal government to pay all back taxes, and based on estimates we paid our quarterly taxes in advance.

~LESSONS LEARNED~

1. Pay taxes on time

2. As a small business, if you withhold paying your taxes, the federal government can force you to go out of business by attaching liens to your financial accounts, preventing you from conducting business

3. The whole process can be very embarrassing

4. Not paying your taxes is one of the biggest mistakes that small businesses make

~HOW TO INTEGRATE YOUR PERSONAL AND PROFESSIONAL LIFE~ I spend 80 percent of my time on my professional life and 20 percent of my time on my personal life. When I was younger and raising my children the split was 50/50. My children are all grown now and on their own. I have been married for 32 years, so your relationship with your spouse becomes less intense as you grow old together.

The 80 percent of my time that I spend on my professional life is broken down into 60 percent of my time working on relationships associated with my business. The other 20 percent is spent on logistics of the business and travel.

Because so much of my time is spent away from my personal life, every time I return home it is like a honeymoon – it keeps the romance alive.

I love my work so much that I do not consider it to be work. I get tremendous enjoyment from it. Working for me is like playing.

~FORMULA FOR SUCCESS~ Have a large vision for what you want, but think small. All success begins with small steps. Have dreams, have patience and the willingness to do the work. All great things in life start as a seed. That is, they start small. Most people are not willing to do the work. In a nutshell, the formula for success is large vision, think small and do the work.

~MAJOR REGRET~ A major regret that I always have is, knowing that I will never have as much time as I will need to do all the things that I want to do. I will always want more time. Because of this, I live each day as if I am going to die tomorrow. This keeps me on my toes and makes me more productive. I know that I am going to die because that's inevitable, but I regret it because I cannot do all the things that I want to do.

~FAVOURITE QUOTE~ My favourite quote is "First things first, second things never." This is a quote that I made up and I always tell people because I believe in it. Whatever you have to do, break it down into steps and work on the first step. Your only focus is on that first step until it's completed. You have to have the discipline to focus on the thing that is in front of you. The second step now becomes your next first step so there is never a second step because you are focused on one thing at a time. If your goal is to write a book, what steps do you have to take to make that goal a reality? Do only one thing at a time because you can only walk down one road at a time, so walk down that road. **FOCUS, FOCUS, FOCUS!**

137

~INFLUENTIAL BOOK~ There are two books that had a profound impact on my life – *Winning With People* by John Maxwell and *Destruction of Black Civilization: Great Issues of a Race from 4500 B.C. to 2000 A.D.* by Chancellor Williams. *Winning With People* is about building relationships and is a seminal text to the work that I do – everything is about relationships. *Destruction of Black Civilization* helped me to understand what happened in Africa, what happened to what was once a great continent.

ANDREA NIERENBERG
BUILDING RELATIONSHIPS

"With integrity, nothing else matters and without integrity, nothing else matters." -Author Unknown

~CHALLENGE~ As a small company, the challenge is always getting in the door to a large, branded company.

~RESOLUTION~ I build relationships one person at a time. I meet people through my programs and at speaking/networking events. I nurture these relationships and doors have opened.

~LESSONS LEARNED~

1. Be reliable, trustworthy, always follow-up, and be a great listener

2. Most people have some of the above traits, yet I have realized that to be successful you have to have all of them

138

~HOW TO INTEGRATE YOUR PERSONAL AND PROFESSIONAL LIFE~ People who I meet professionally often turn into friends. I really love what I do, so it doesn't feel like work. So, I live my work, however I do have a lot of balance in my life.

~FORMULA FOR SUCCESS~ According to Vidal Sassoon, "The only place where success comes before work is in the dictionary." To become successful, you have to be determined, reliable, consistent, and keep looking for the goal that you want to achieve.

~MAJOR REGRET~ You always think about what might have been, but I have learned to go with the cards that I have been dealt. Fifteen years ago, I was in a serious car accident. I broke 40 bones. At the time, I felt really sorry for myself, but I also learned a lot during that period. You always have to find the silver lining in the clouds.

~FAVOURITE QUOTE~ My favourite quote is something I read and keep on my desk, "With integrity, nothing else matters and without integrity, nothing else matters."

~INFLUENTIAL BOOK~ *How to Win Friends and Influence People* by Dale Carnegie had a profound impact on my life. For the past 15 years, I have been reading this book once a year and each time I get something new from it. The book is based on common sense and communication. Essentially, the book tells you how to be more mindful.

HEATHER RESNICK
STATING CLEAR EXPECTATIONS

"I was doing what I wanted to do and a dream was coming through and that above anything else, made it worthwhile to me."
-Terry Fox

~CHALLENGE~ My biggest business challenge was making assumptions that self-publishing would be a seamless, mostly stress-free experience (it can never be completely stress less because it is like having a baby - there is always eager anticipation and some anxiety.) For example, I was never sure of when my book would be ready because I did not have a firm date in writing. Verbally I was told it would be various times and I believed that to be so. As a result I lost out on potential business either because I could not attend an event or at an event I did not have the book in my hands.

~RESOLUTION~ I resolved my challenge by stating firm expectations in writing, having all parties agree and sign. I also expressed the importance of why my expectations had to be met and penalties if they were not met. When I took control of the situation, things started to happen.

139

~LESSONS LEARNED~

1. Thoroughly research your publishing options while you are in the writing process

2. Use a book shepherd to guide you through the process if you are a novice author

3. Never assume anything - make sure everything is clearly spelled out in writing

4. Take the time to consider the comfort level of the proposal and the prospective people you will be working with before you proceed

5. Like anything else in a self-business it is up to the author to be on top of all the details

6. Honest communication is imperative to a successful relationship with everyone involved in your production process

~HOW TO INTEGRATE YOUR PERSONAL AND PROFESSIONAL LIFE~To ensure that I balance my life, I turn off my computer every evening at 6:00 p.m. and it's off all weekend. I also do only the things that I really enjoy doing. To integrate the two worlds, I attend professional events such as workshops where I create a long-term network of relationships of friends and colleagues. I earnestly take interest in the other person and try to provide them with valuable information.

~FORMULA FOR SUCCESS~ Success is to believe in what you're doing, with passion and exuberance. Be prepared to work hard. Craft a support system of people who will affirm your dreams, share your values and goals and be constructively honest. Remember, success is in the eye of the beholder.

~MAJOR REGRET~ I regret spending money on things before carefully researching them, which ended up costing me substantially more money. I simply didn't think things through. It is very important to always have a plan, talk to others and learn from their mistakes. For example, I did not check out my web site options thoroughly and I probably spent almost a thousand dollars too much. After the fact, I discovered a service that was both cost-efficient and effective.

~FAVOURITE QUOTE~ I like "I was doing what I wanted to do and a dream was coming through and that above anything else, made it worthwhile to me" by Terry Fox, from the book *Terry Fox His Story* by Leslie Scrivener, because it shows the importance of believing in your dreams.

~INFLUENTIAL BOOK~ The book that had a profound impact on me is *Still Me* by Christopher Reeve (he played Superman in the movies). I read this book about a year after I had cancer for the second time. The book talks about Christopher's hope. Reading in between the lines I got the bigger picture of understanding what makes people have hope.

140

CHRIS WIDENER
MAKING A STRATEGIC PARTNERSHIP WORK

"Far better it is to dare mighty things, to win glorious triumphs, even though checkered by failure, than to take rank with those poor spirits who neither enjoy or suffer much because, they live in the gray twilight that knows not neither victory nor defeat."

-Teddy Roosevelt

~CHALLENGE~ At a certain point in my career, I realized that I was doing both the writing and speaking as well as product development and marketing. Even though I was pretty good at it, my challenge was to take my career to the next level. I realized that what I needed to do was to find another person or company that I could partner with, who had skills to complement me in areas where they were strong and I was weak.

~RESOLUTION~ I took a number of months to look at, and pursue individuals and companies. I then began to work on the partnership ideas with them, and eventually found the right person and the right company to partner with, to develop Chris Widener International.

141

~LESSONS LEARNED~

1. Don't only look at a company's reputation, but look at its people. You have to find a person that you can trust. A company is only as good as the people you deal with. In addition to the people having a high character, they must also have the skill set and the skill level

2. Make sure that you do all of the due diligence prior to going into the partnership. Make sure that you understand the other party's expectations of you, and make sure that they understand your expectations of them. The more upfront work that you do, the better off you are after the deal is struck

3. Make sure that you are both flexible, and that the business relationship is advantageous to both parties. If both sides want to have a long-term relationship they have to consider each other's interest.

~HOW TO INTEGRATE YOUR PERSONAL AND PROFESSIONAL LIFE~ They are integrated – my office is in my home. I do not feel like I work hard because the things that I do I love to do. I love my work. When I travel on speaking engagements around the country, technically it's work because I am networking and meeting people but it never feels like work because I really enjoy meeting people. I guess the way I integrate my personal and professional life is through my perspective because I do what I love to do and it makes what other people would consider to be work not feel like work to me.

~FORMULA FOR SUCCESS~ According to Brian Tracy, "Do what you resolve to do." I think that that's interesting because if you break that up it boils down to knowing what you want to do. And, what you resolve to do is what you thought about, which should be born out of your passion, strength, desires and capabilities. But, it is one thing to resolve to do something, and it's another thing to do what you resolve to do. So, decide what you want to do and act on it.

Small steps daily will take you further ahead of people with lofty goals who do nothing.

True success comes from having balanced achievements in all the areas of your life – financially, emotionally, relationally, spiritually, physically.

~MAJOR REGRET~ Earlier on in my career I didn't learn how to properly interact with other people. I didn't try hard enough to make relationships work. People whom I did business with, who may not have done it exactly the way I wanted, instead of seeking common ground to make it work, I severed the relationships without giving them the chance.

~FAVOURITE QUOTE~ I like "Far better it is to dare mighty things, to win glorious triumphs, even though checkered by failure, than to take rank with those poor spirits who neither enjoy or suffer much because, they live in the gray twilight that knows not neither victory nor defeat" by Teddy Roosevelt because it reminds me that it's better to try and fail than it is to never try. You are a better person if you are willing to take risks and do your best even though you may fail sometimes.

~INFLUENTIAL BOOK~ The book that has impacted my life the most is *The Holy Bible*. It has the stories of the greatest triumphs and the greatest tragedies. It shows the human condition and the human potential. It introduces us to a man - Jesus - whose life and teachings have transformed the world and countless lives. It teaches faith, hope and love. Its teachings have driven the expansion of western culture, the building of countless millions of hospitals, schools, and orphanages to name just a few of the ways that *The Holy Bible* and its teachings have changed our world. Most importantly for me, when I was a wandering young man, drifting aimlessly but in the wrong direction, it corrected my path and pointed me in the direction I continue in today. It taught me how to handle my relationships, money, work, my family, my mind and myself. It taught me how to live for others rather than for myself. It taught me how to find peace, no matter what storms may face me.

143

144

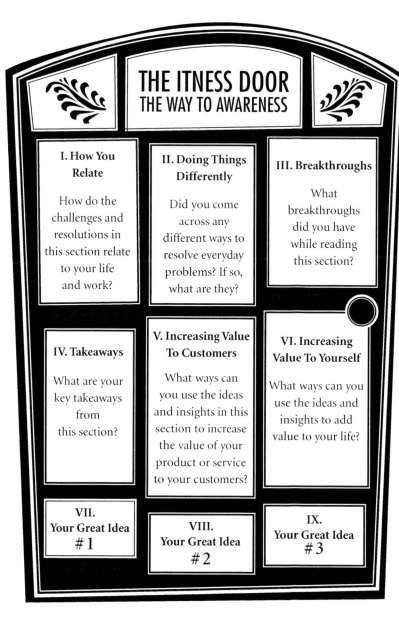

145

146

FAVOURITE QUOTES

"Be the change you want to see in the world." ~Mahatma Ghandi

"For things to change, we must change." ~Jim Rohn

"If you don't like where you are, change what you are."
~Henry Knight Miller

"For what are your possessions but things you keep and guard for fear you might need them tomorrow? And tomorrow, what shall tomorrow bring to the over-prudent dog burying bones in the trackless sand as he follows the pilgrims to the holy city?" ~Kahlil Gibran

"There is nothing to fear but fear itself." ~Franklin D. Roosevelt

"Walking toward the fear is always a good idea. You're bigger than it is; you just don't know it yet" ~Jon Carroll

*"Our deepest fear is not that we are inadequate. Our deepest fear is that we are powerful beyond measure. It is our light, not our darkness that most frightens us. We ask ourselves, "Who am I to be brilliant, gorgeous, talented, fabulous?" Actually, who are you not to be? You are a child of God. Your playing small does not serve the world.
There is nothing enlightened about shrinking so that other people won't feel insecure around you. We are all meant to shine, as children do. We were born to make manifest the glory of God that is within us. It is not just in some of us; it is in everyone. And as we let our own light shine, we unconsciously give other people permission to do the same. As we are liberated from our own fear, our presence automatically liberates others."*
~MarianneWilliamson

"Labour for learning before you grow old, for learning is better than silver and gold. Silver and gold will vanish away, but a good education will never decay." ~Popular Jamaican Saying

"An investment in knowledge always pay the best interest"
~Benjamin Franklin

147

"Those who cannot learn from history are doomed to repeat it."
~George Santayana

"Never doubt that a small group of thoughtful, committed citizens can change the world. Indeed, it is the only thing that ever has."
~Margaret Meade

"What stirs the mind or touches the heart, will undoubtedly move the feet." ~Donald Murphy

"Generals plan for months on the way they are going to fight the battle and then ten minutes into the battle the plans are useless and those who have the most passion win." ~European General, First World War

"Far better it is to dare mighty things, to win glorious triumphs, even though checkered by failure, than to take rank with those poor spirits who neither enjoy or suffer much because they live in the gray twilight that knows not neither victory nor defeat."
~Teddy Roosevelt

"I can do all things through Him who strengthens me."
~Philippians 4:13

"It ain't over till it's over." ~Yogi Berra

"Nothing can resist a human will that will stake even its existence on the extent of its purpose." ~Benjamin Disraeli

"First things first, second things never" ~George Fraser

"Bring me a good one-armed economist. I'm fed up with being told that on one hand.., but that on the other ..." ~Harry Truman

"Success is not a place at which one arrives but rather the spirit with which one undertakes and continues the journey." ~Alex Noble

"There are only two things you need for success: courage and ignorance." ~Gabriel Draven (Inspired by Mark Twain's quote)

"We can't solve problems by using the same kind of thinking we used when we created them." ~Albert Einstein

"Only the best is good enough." ~Author Unknown

"Let gratitude be your attitude." ~Author Unknown

"The place God calls you to is the place where your deep gladness and the world's deep hunger meet." ~Frederick Beuchner

"Miracles rest not so much upon healing power coming suddenly near us from afar, but upon our perceptions being made finer, so that for the moment our eyes can see and our ears can hear what has been there around us always." ~Willa Cather

"I was doing what I wanted to do and a dream was coming through and that above anything else, made it worthwhile to me." ~ Terry Fox

149

"I believe it, and so I see it" -Marshall McLuhan

"If you can keep your head when all about you are losing theirs and blaming it on you." ~ Rudyard Kipling

"With integrity, nothing else matters and without integrity, nothing else matters." ~ Author Unknown

"Worrying about something is like paying interest on a debt you don't even know if you owe." ~ Mark Twain

"Eternity is a mere moment, just long enough for a joke even if it is sardonic" ~ Hermann Hesse

"There is no way it is, there is only the way you say it is. The universe hasn't made up its mind about you. It only knows what you show it today. You are the Inventor; your life is the invention. You get to make it up, so make it up good." ~ Gail Blanke

"The most powerful weapon on earth is the human soul on fire"
~ Ferdinand Foch

"We are all caught in an inescapable network of mutuality, tied into a single garment of destiny, whatever affects one directly, affect all indirectly" -Martin Luther King (Inspired by Ghandi)

"We are made to live together because of the interrelated structure of reality" ~ Martin Luther King

"Insanity is doing the same thing over and over but expecting to get a different result."
~Popularly attributed to Albert Einstein & Benjamin Franklin

SECTION 3
THE DECONSTRUCTION

 INSIGHTS

Real people! Real stories! Real wisdom! Real success! The interviewees are everyday people; people whom you can relate to. Their stories are very interesting and instructive, and you can achieve their successes because you can see yourself in them. Although they are everyday people, there is a "specialness" about them. From their stories, you realize that they know that life is more than just about them. They really understand what life is about. They "get it".

Most of the interviewees do not know each other, but their answers show a connectedness among them.

To demonstrate the connections, sit back, relax and enjoy the play, *Tales of People Who Get It.*

THE PLAY

TALES OF PEOPLE WHO GET IT

Opening Night

The Stage Setting

The only set decoration is a white backdrop with a red and white bull's eye target off centre to the right. The middle of the target has a deep red, heart-shaped book with what appears to be two eyes on the front cover, looking deep into your soul.

ACT I
Scene I

Setting The Scene – Background Information

The actors, Nanci Govinder and Seaton McLean come on the stage and the story unfolds. They explain that it came across loud and clear that people are our greatest assets. Both Nanci and Seaton were involved, separately, in downsizing at their companies. Their attitudes toward people made all the difference in the world. In Nanci's case, shortly after the downsizing, her company had to exhibit at a major medical conference and her colleagues came through for her.

~Nanci Govinder~

I pulled salespeople with sound product knowledge out of the field in the United States, as well as product managers, company veterans and so on to come and help. The new product managers that were hired in new offices and those that were still working their termination period in their previous jobs took vacation and came to the conference to help out. I explained the severity and urgency of the situation and there was no "us" versus "them."

She further adds second lesson learned.

If your intention is clear and honest, people will rally around you and unify toward a common goal or vision.

Seaton talks about a life lesson.

~Seaton McLean~

As long as you are honest you can resolve 99 percent of all situations amicably and without regret.

Scene II

Seaton and Nanci leave the stage. Samy Chong comes on stage and the other actors for this scene line up. In Samy Chong's challenge, he talks about the sense of hopelessness that he felt because of the uncertainty of where his restaurant business was going. He reminisces!

~Samy Chong ~

I remember a dishwasher who was making $7 or $8 an hour came up to me and told me that if I didn't have the money to pay him for the next couple of months, that it would be okay. The faith and trust of my staff, which I had cared for in the past, pulled me through this very difficult time and ensured the protection of the restaurant.

Suzanne Gibson thoughtfully adds to what Samy is saying, in her lessons learned.

~Suzanne Gibson~

I recognized and learned how important it was to "cobble"

together dedicated staff. We didn't have the money to pay the staff, but we all worked part-time, and gave up our hearts to the idea – the key team was essential – they were skilled, passionate and highly motivated – nothing can be done without a team approach… I learned about the power of people and how all these "angels" fell from the sky and participated in giving to the cause – things only ever happen because many hands till the soil.

Prudence Brown in her lessons learned.

~Prudence Brown~

I learned about the importance of communication, and the need to involve other parties from an early stage, in the decision-making process, in situations in which they are affected, and recognize their views and input.

Gail Blanke joins her on stage, and pipes out her lesson learned.

154

~Gail Blanke~

Trust, and anticipate that other people will be as committed as you are.

John Gardner continues in the same scene and talks about his lesson learned.

~John Gardner~

A manager does not accomplish much working on his own.

As the story continues to unfold, Simon Grant explains using his lesson learned.

~Simon Grant~

Without your colleagues you are nothing and trying to truly understand them as individuals is the most respectful thing you can do as a leader. And mutual respect provides the foundation for motivation in almost all cases.

Gloria Lattanzio thickens the plot, in her formula for success.

~Gloria Lattanzio~

You really do need to surround yourself with good people, and recognize that you cannot do anything by yourself, so you need to have people around you. And, you need to have people around you who complement what you bring, because your own weaknesses are made irrelevant by other people's strengths.

ACT II
Scene I

Gloria starts off a new act and scene in the play.

~Gloria Lattanzio~

Recognize that everybody wants to do a good job, and your job is to find out what the talent is that everybody brings, to help them become successful, because their success is your success.

Stephen Abram comes on stage. In his resolution, he explains his aim.

~Stephen Abram~

[Our aim is] to make our clients more successful which will make us more successful.

Janice Lawrence-Clarke reinforces what the others are saying using a lesson learned.

~Janice Lawrence-Clarke~

…My success depends on the success of others. I learned to zero in and treat myself as one of my clients.

Janice exits the stage.

ACT III
Scene I

In his third lesson learned, Samy Chong talks about passion and purpose.

~Samy Chong~

Make sure that what we do is in alignment with our purpose on this earth, and hopefully that purpose is in alignment with our passion. And if you have the purpose and passion, you basically have a vocation that truly serves humanity.

155

In that same vein, Stephanie MacKendrick in her response to the formula for success says the same thing in a different way.

~Stephanie MacKendrick~

What you're good at and what you enjoy doing are not always the same. I think that if you can align what you enjoy doing, and what you're good at, your chances of success and having really high impact is much better. All of this requires a very strategic outlook on everything that you do.

Ann Kirkland adds to what Stephanie is saying, in her response to the formula for success.

~Ann Kirkland~

The great key for anyone is finding your own personal vocation. There is no guarantee that if you find it, it's going to work, but I think that finding something that incorporates who you are, your own personal nature with something that feels worthwhile is very satisfying… Knowing who you are and what your gifts are, your limitations, and then finding a way to put that to use that is a benefit to the world, somehow helps.

In Gabriel Draven's response to integrating his personal and professional life, he takes his answer one step further.

~Gabriel Draven~

I had to try and figure out how to integrate my personal value set with a way to make money, and I finally did it.

Back to Samy Chong in his answer to the formula for success.

~Samy Chong ~

If I were to describe the formula for success as a diagram, I would use three overlapping circles. The first circle would represent what the world needs. Circle two would represent your greatest gifts, passion and purpose, and circle three would represent where the money is. Where the circles overlap in the middle is truly what you came here on earth to do – honouring your purpose, honouring what the world needs and following where the money or energy is.

ACT IV
Scene I

Setting The Scene – Background Information

Another important connection emerged as Asha McLeod talks about her challenge.

~Asha McLeod~

What I found most challenging was that I was constantly doing all I could do to train [my employees] to be the best stylists they could be. This involved countless hours of professional training, personal and emotional support. The end result would always be that I would have trained and developed successful, confident stylists. So successful and confident that they would always believe they were capable of more than working for me, and would leave our salon, usually taking our clientele that they had built up as a result of working with us.

157

Oliver Campbell takes the stage. In his second lesson learned he explains.

~Oliver Campbell~

The loss of a client is not necessarily a negative. New business opportunities constantly arise and the loss of a client may in fact allow you to accept new business.

Asha ponders for a while, and continues in her resolution.

~Asha McLeod~

I changed my perspective and motivating factors for why I teach them. Instead of teaching them to be successful because it would be better for my business, I now train them believing I am helping them to become better people. I also train them not expecting gratitude in return, and knowing they will move on eventually.

Now in her response to integrating her personal and professional life, she adds.

~Asha McLeod~

I believe I have been blessed with my skills and talent because I have a duty to share them with humanity. I see myself as a key that enables others to unlock their abilities and become better and more beautiful people. To me I find life more fulfilling and work more rewarding by viewing the world and living life this way.

The audience see a progression as the story unfolds and you realize that what Oliver says is true. In Asha's case, she loses staff and clients, but that isn't a bad thing because her purpose in life is to teach people a unique technique that she has developed based on years of research. Staff leaving and taking clientele with them, allows her to fulfill her purpose in life because she gets to train new employees in her technique. She also gets the opportunity to take on new clients in her salon.

ACT V
Scene I

Setting The Scene – Background Information

The whole idea of journey came up several times in the stories. The actors and actresses referred to inner and outer journey and sometimes the journey was implied while other times it was mentioned explicitly. As the play unfolds, you'll see how different actors provide the same answers to different questions and the same answers to the same questions.

The ACT starts off with Anthea Rossouw and Suzanne Gibson talking about going out into nature as a way of integrating their personal and professional lives. This is an explicit outer journey, though they never actually use the word.

~Suzanne Gibson~

To balance myself, I have a physical fitness training program, a meditation and spiritual practice, I get out in nature and I try to keep the people in my life, who I love, close to me. If I feed myself personally I am much better professionally.

~Anthea Rossouw~

Peace descends on me when I am outside in nature, and the environment gives me strength. It gives me the strength and energy to interact with people on both the personal and private level. When I watch the trees and hear the breeze, I know that there is a bigger purpose.

Scene II

Lea Chambers comes on stage. In her response to the formula for success she talks about an implied journey you take as your life unfolds.

~Lea Chambers~

Success is the awareness in each moment of who you ARE and the celebration of your Unfolding as you go through your Life, regardless of changing circumstances.

Samy Chong in his formula for success continues with the whole notion of unfolding and actually uses the word journey.

~Samy Chong~

Once you signal to the universe where you are going, you just need to let go and allow things to unfold. And the journey that I've been on is exactly that, leaving a career where I was doing quite well and moving into another where I had no idea how I was going to do.

Samy expands on the journey argument when he talks about influential books.

~Samy Chong~

The Celestine Prophecy... started me on this journey and allowed me to really open my eyes to what this journey on earth is really about... I like [*Power vs. Force*] because it maps out the skill of consciousness journey of where each of us are at, and directs us to what the next step will lead us to.

Scene III

Gloria Lattanzio and Simon Grant take the stage and talk about journey when they explain why they like their favourite quotations.

~Gloria Lattanzio~

Life is a long journey that we go on, and we need to appreciate and recognize the lessons that we learn on that journey, and be able to see whatever lessons experience teaches us so that we become better, and leave the world a better place than when we came into it.

~Simon Grant~

Enjoying life is not about enjoying and having passion for the achievement of goals, but about enjoying and having passion for the journey itself.

Tonya Lee Williams comes on stage and talks about journey in her response to regrets.

~Tonya Lee Williams~

I love the journey of my life, and wouldn't wish to change a single moment for fear that I may also change and lose the wonderful moments.

Prudence Brown talks about success as it relates to journey in her summary of books that influence.

~Prudence Brown~

Your Roadmap for Success emphasizes that success is not wealth, power or happiness, and not something one acquires, or achieves, but a journey that you take your whole life.

Asha in her formula for success adds context to success and journey.

~Asha McLeod~

Keep in mind that success is never a final destination, but a journey, and as long as you are committed to lifelong learning, and passionate about your work, success is inevitable.

The actors and actresses take their bow.

***

These are some of the many connections, but the drama continues to unfold on the stage.

THE END

For the opening night there was a special surprise waiting for the audience. The director of *Tales of People Who Get It* was making a special appearance for an impromptu 15-minute question and answer session.

The attendees roared because they were delighted. Taking the initiative, one audience member worked her way close to the stage because she simply had to have her burning question answered. Two others noticed what she was doing and followed her lead. For showing initiative they got rewarded. Their questions were answered.

Audience Member 1

What are five key things that you want people to take away?

Director

These are the five keys things that I would like you to take away:

1. Everything is connected, we are all connected, what affects one, affects all

2. Take the time to build the right network of people who complement your skills because no one succeeds alone

3. Slow down, take the time to experience and enjoy life, focus on what you're doing and make lifelong learning a priority

4. Get to know who you are – what you like and don't like, what your strengths and weaknesses are and discover what your life purpose is

Audience Member 2

If there were one thing that you wanted us to do when we leave, what would it be?

Director

Become a success in all five areas of your life: economic/financial, social, health, business/career and personal. This allows you to live a more fulfilled life.

Audience Member 3

How would you summarize *Tales of People Who Get It?*

Director

Tales of People Who Get It is based on the book of the same name. It's a story about how ordinary people - with the same challenges and struggles we all face - succeed. It's about recapturing your passion, focusing on what you want and being a perpetual learner to make yourself more valuable. It's about living in the moment, living the life you were meant to live, a life with purpose, and enjoying your life and work.

GETTING IT

Now you've seen the connections. The interviewees are connected by their thoughts, words, actions and belief systems. Focus, learning and passion kept on cropping up throughout the interviews.

Who "gets it?" Are we born with "it?" Can "it" be thrust upon us? Or, is "it" something that we acquire?

Some people "get "it" and others don't. Some of those who don't "get it," never will. Those who "get it" fall along a continuum, so some people have more of "it" than others. As the interviewees share their stories, you see how they learn, grow and evolve and move up to a higher level of "itness". Some people who "get it" can lose their "itness" if they lose the qualities of someone who "gets it."

162

THE ITNESS CONTINUUM

|——|

"NON-ITNESS"   "ULTIMATE ENLIGHTENMENT"

"It" cannot be thrust upon you, and if you're born with "it," you evolve as you grow and your "itness" comes out. For those of us who acquire "it," as we evolve and grow, we become wiser and more enlightened. The highest point on the "itness" continuum is enlightenment. Enlightenment is the ultimate achievement in and of itself.

PROFILE OF SOMEONE WHO "GETS IT"

And so, pulling from the stories, people who "get it" understand that learning is not an end, but an endless process. They invest in themselves by making personal and professional development a priority, always taking courses, reading broadly, observing and making sure that they look at what's been done before, not reinventing the wheel. They practice active listening and know the difference between listening and hearing.

Recognizing that life isn't just about them, and that there is a higher purpose, they understand the value of relationships, knowing that no one succeeds alone. They refuse to stick to the status quo, always looking for new and innovative ways to do things, finding creative ways to solve problems by thinking deeply and differently and adapting to different situations.

They have a zest for life, loving and enjoying their work. They really get to know themselves, recognizing their vulnerabilities and finding ways to address them. Taking a holistic approach to life, they can see the bigger picture, always taking action, committing to goals and following through, while focusing only on the task at hand.

From the profile of someone who "gets it", 13 clues emerge that let you know when you're dealing with someone who "gets it." These clues are ItnessPoints.

A BAKER'S DOZEN ITNESSPOINTS
CLUES THAT SOMEONE "GETS IT"

1. Learns continuously/Reads voraciously

2. Listens and hears

3. Understands that there is a higher purpose, and life isn't just about me

4. Cultivates relationships, surrounds himself/herself with the "right" people

5. Refuses to be satisfied with the status quo

6. Thinks deeply and differently

7. Adapts to different situations

8. Loves and enjoys work and life

9. Knows himself/herself

10. Recognizes vulnerabilities

11. Takes a holistic approach to life

12. Focuses on the task at hand

13. Commits and follow through

163

People who "get it" had a unique way of adapting the interview questions to their situations. They answer the questions in ways that make sense to them. Their varying interpretations make their responses interesting, reflect personality, and help us to get to know them and better understand their belief systems.

INTEGRATING LIFE

When it comes to integrating their personal and professional lives, the tone of the responses could be grouped into soft, strong and forceful. No matter what the tone, the messages are very clear.

Some people admitted that it was difficult and sometimes a struggle to integrate their personal and professional life. Despite the difficulty, they have found techniques that help them to lead more balanced lives. Others, who once had difficulty, got better as they grew older, which may be a function of where they are now in their careers. Other interviewees indicated that they have one life, but many aspects to it, so the value set that they use in one, they use in all.

The people who work for themselves have an easier time of integrating their personal and professional life. One important discovery is that even though your life is integrated, doesn't necessarily mean that it's balanced.

Some responses were very detailed so you could quite easily replicate the instructions if you chose to. Some got right to the point and others were more philosophical. George Fraser provided a detailed response: "I spend 80 percent of my time on my professional life and 20 percent of my time on my personal life. When I was younger and raising my children the split was 50/50. My children are all grown now and on their own. I have been married for 32 years, so your relationship with your spouse becomes less intense as you grow old together. The 80 percent of my time that I spend on my professional life is broken down into 60 percent of my time working on relationships associated with my business. The other 20 percent is spent on logistics of the business and travel. Because so much of my time is spent away from my personal life, every time I return home it is like a honeymoon – it keeps the romance alive."

Joe Martin in his response explains, "My wife would say that I do not integrate my personal and professional life as well as I should, but I think that I have always done a reasonable job. We have four children and seven grandchildren… We are also very involved in our grandchildren's lives – we make time to watch their hockey games. I always make time for my family, and the trick is to do the unexpected and not just the expected."

Peter Bouffard was more philosophical in his response: "In the past, my personal and professional life used to be very different, but now, I live what I do. I am doing who I am."

REGRETS

In life we often have experiences that are regrettable. Some people choose to use them as learning tools while others waste time worrying about them. Looking back over their lives so far, the interviewees reflected on their regrets, or lack thereof.

Most of the regrets fall under career/business, education, relationships, wisdom, and no regrets. Most of the interviewees either did not have any regrets or simply chose not to focus on them.

Anthea Rossouw wishes that she had started her business much sooner instead of waiting on others to help her to get her message out. Purdy Crawford regrets having been so accommodating early on in his career, compromising his opinions to make some of his clients happy.

165

If Peter Bouffard could live his life over he would definitely spend more time building relationships, instead of thinking that he has all the answers. Recognizing the value of education, some interviewees wished they had more formal education or studied more interesting things. People who "get it" know that learning is paramount to success.

SUCCESS FORMULA

Is there a universal formula for success? *The Oxford English Reference Dictionary* defines success as:

1. The accomplishment of an aim; a favourable outcome

2. The attainment of wealth, fame or position

3. A thing or person that turns out well

Earl Nightingale, a successful broadcast personality, who authored more than 7,000 radio and television commentaries while he was alive, defines success in *The Strangest Secret* as "the progressive realization of a worthy ideal. If he is not doing that, he's a failure… A success is anyone who is doing deliberately a predetermined job, because that's what he decided to do… deliberately."

How did the interviewees become successful? What wisdom do they have to share? What ingredients are in their formulas for success? The formulas for success are as diverse as the interviewees. The responses range from the philosophical to the specific.

Despite this, there were ingredients in the formula, as well as traits that successful people possess. Some people defined success so that you could understand their frame of reference.

Maria Nemeth who founded the Academy for Coaching Excellence defines success as "Do what you say you're going to do in life, and do it with clarity, focus, ease and grace." Claire Hoy, a journalist who wrote a number one New York Times Bestseller, looks at success in terms of "doing what you like, and enjoying the lifestyle that comes about." Author Heather Resnick says success is "to believe in what you're doing with passion and exuberance." Lea Chambers, a marketing specialist, defines success as "the awareness in each moment of who you ARE and the celebration of your Unfolding as you go through your Life, regardless of changing circumstances." Success is "getting to know who you are and designing and living the life you desire; by overcoming your fears and ridding yourself of the mask you created," says Nanci Govinder, a personal mastery instructor.

All of these definitions demonstrate that people who "get it" do not define success in the usual way, which focuses solely or mostly on the financial aspect.

Below are the ingredients in the formula for success, and the traits of a successful person pulled from the interviews.

TABLE 1: INGREDIENTS IN THE FORMULA FOR SUCCESS

INGREDIENTS	
Desire	Commitment
Action	Focus
Reliability	Persistence
Determination	Consistency
Continuous learning	Passion
Education	Capabilities
Patience	Discipline
Hard work	Faith
Listening skills	Trust
Questioning skills	Communication skills
Your personal vocation/what the world needs	

TABLE 2: TRAITS OF A SUCCESSFUL PERSON

TRAITS	
Humility	Dignity
Courage	Integrity
Lifelong learner	Charisma
Tenacious	Having a broad perspective
Action-oriented	Ability to overcome
Kindness	challenges
Supportive	Understanding
Respect for others	Ability to work with others
	Ability to create product/ service in demand

Using the various formulas for success from the interviewees, we could develop a generic success model, which could be customized according to one's unique situation.

167

TABLE 3: PEOPLE WHO "GET IT" SUCCESS MODEL

STAGE	PROCESS	RESULT
Definition	1. How do you define success? 2. What does success mean to you? NOTE: Make sure that your definition encompasses all aspects of your life	**Personal Success Definition**
Evaluation	Based on your Personal Success Definition: 3. What do you want to do with your life? 4. What's your vision? 5. What do you "need" to do to become successful? 6. What has prevented you from becoming successful? 7. Develop specific strategies in advance to use when one of these obstacles arises 8. What lessons did you learn from these challenges? 9. What are the things that you need to do to increase your chances for success? 10. What are some services and products that the world needs? Develop short, medium and long-term goals based on your answers to the above questions. In addition, write out your life's purpose, which should also come out of this process	**Personal Success Action Plan**
Action Steps	11. What personal action steps do you have to take to successfully implement your Personal Success Action Plan? Group your actions into business/career, economic, personal, health and social. Attach timelines to accomplishing each action	**Personal Success Action Steps**
Maintenance	12. Now that you've attained success, how do you maintain it?	**Personal Success Maintenance Plan**

A successful person is a continuous learner, where learning doesn't have to be formal, as in a classroom taking a course, instead it could be learning from a book. People who "get it" are leaders and leaders are readers.

INFLUENTIAL BOOKS

Some interviewees were influenced by things other than books – a conversation, mentor, course, an experience and so on - and when you reflect on what they had to say, you can see and understand why they responded the way they did.

For example, when Gail Blanke was 10 years old she saw the play *Our Town*, which made her realize the importance of telling others how much she loves and appreciates them. At this age, she recognized that the play was about "seizing the moment and living life fully in the moment." From that time she always let people know how she feels about them.

When Suzanne Gibson was in her early twenties, just starting out her career, her mentor, Ratna Omidvar took her under her wings and told her that she could accomplish anything. This increased Suzanne's belief in herself. Ratna also opened doors, which catapulted Suzanne into positions and opportunities that she wouldn't have gotten otherwise. Being mentored by such a positive role model impacted Suzanne in the way she works, and in the way she understands how to support others in their work. Being mentored, influenced Suzanne and she understands the importance of mentoring others.

169

Using the categories used by booksellers to group books, the deconstruction showed that business books had less influence on people who "get it" than self-help, spiritual, fictional or cultural studies books. Only four business books made it on the list - *Beyond Certainty: The Changing Worlds of Organizations*, *The Entrepreneurial Journey In Jamaica: When Policies Derail*, *Winning With People* and *Your Roadmap for Success*. Some books fell into more than one group.

So, what is it about these books that influenced the lives of people who get it? According to Mortimer Adler and Charles Van Doren in *How To Read A Book: The Classic Guide to Intelligent Reading*, there are three reasons why someone reads: for entertainment, information or understanding. The authors also state that, "Enlightenment is achieved only when, in addition to knowing what an authors says, you know what he means and why he says it."

Books that influence provide interviewees with a deeper level of understanding about something. They take full ownership of the contents of the book and make it a part of themselves. They know how to interpret and apply the contents of the books to their unique situations. The books enlighten people who "get it" – they understand what the authors are saying and why they are saying what they say.

READING LIST: BOOKS THAT INFLUENCE PEOPLE WHO GET IT

1. Dante Alighieri, *Divine Comedy*
2. Maya Angelou, *All God's Children Need Traveling Shoes*
3. Maya Angelou, *I Know Why The Caged Bird Sings*
4. Venice Bloodworth, *Key To Yourself*
5. Gerald Brenan, *South From Granada*
6. Dale Carnegie, *How To Win Friends And Influence People*
7. Paul L. Chen-Young, *The Entrepreneurial Journey in Jamaica*
8. Ron Chernow, *Alexander Hamilton: The Year That Rocked The World*
9. Stephen Covey, *The Seven Habits Of Highly Effective People*
10. Anthony de Mello, *The Way To Love*
11. Creflo A Dollar & Taffi L. Dollar, *The Successful Family*
12. Marilyn French, *The Women's Room*
13. Kahlil Gibran, *The Prophet*
14. Germaine Greer, *The Female Eunuch*
15. Charles Handy, *Beyond Certainty: The Changing Worlds of Organizations*
16. David Hawkins, *Power vs. Force*
17. Cheri Huber, *That Which You Are Seeking Is Causing You To Seek*
18. Maxwell Maltz, *The New Psycho-Cybernetics*
19. Marcel Mauss, *The Gift: The Form And Reason For Exchange in Archaic Societies*
20. John C. Maxwell, *Winning With People*
21. John C. Maxwell, *Your Roadmap For Success*

24. Christopher Reeve, *Still Me*
25. J. M. Roberts, *The Penguin History Of The World*
26. Dr. David J. Schwartz, *The Magic of Thinking Big*
27. Gloria Steinem, *Outrageous Acts And Everyday Rebellions*
28. John Steinbeck, *The Grapes Of Wrath*
29. J. R. R. Tolkien, *The Lord Of The Rings*
30. Kurt Vonnegut, *Slaughterhouse-Five*
31. Neale Donald Walsh, *The Little Soul And The Sun*
32. Chancellor Williams, *The Destruction Of Black Civilization*
33. Paramhansa Yogananda, *Autobiography Of A Yogi*

READING LIST: OTHER BOOKS

1. Mortimer J. Adler & Charles Van Doren, *How to Read A Book*
2. Paul & Gail Dennison, *Brain Gym*
3. Thich Nhat Hanh, *The Miracle of Mindfulness*
4. Earl Nightingale, *The Strangest Secret*

If you read a book a week and you read two of the books on the list, and two other books that you wanted to read, in less than two years, you'll have read all the books on the list. And, you'll have expanded your horizon by reading books that you usually wouldn't read.

The interviewees provided summaries and/or reflections on the books that influenced them. They are grouped for easy reference in Appendix B.

 12 AVIL BECKFORD BASICS:
WHAT I KNOW/HAVE STUMBLED ON

Reading and deconstructing the interviews reminded the author of some important insights that align with what people who "get it" believe and practice.

~LISTEN & HEAR~ It's very important to listen and hear what's being said when someone speaks to you. I always prided myself on having well developed listening skills, and I have often been complimented as well. But, one incident taught me that I could improve.

A few years ago I visited my friend, Julia Watt, who was dying from cancer of the adrenals. During our one-hour visit, I noticed how she hung onto my every word. For that one hour I was the most important person to her. It made me feel very special.

172

~TELL PEOPLE YOU VALUE & APPRECIATE THEM~ After the visit with Julia, I went home and thought about my experience with her and I realized that whenever I was around her, she always behaved in that manner. I wrote her a letter telling her how much I valued and appreciated her friendship. I also mentioned that I noticed that she always made me feel special when I was around her because she always listened to me and actually heard what I had to say. She wrote me and thanked me for my kind words. On a post-it note attached to the card, she encouraged me to read The *Miracle of Mindfulness* by Thich Nhat Hanh. This was my introduction to the art of mindfulness.

I was really happy that I took the time to let her know how I felt about her and that I had noticed the things she did. That visit was the last time that I saw her. Because of that, I am a much better listener, and I am also aware of how little, people listen. Most people prefer to do the talking.

~TAKE A TIME OUT~ I have discovered the value and usefulness of taking time out each day. Just living in our present environment is a major stressor in life. Each day, twice a day, morning and night, I spend at least 15 minutes meditating or "going into the silence." Throughout the day I have check-ins with myself to see how I am doing. If I am anxious or in a panic, I use a technique that Lydia Danner, one of the interviewees, taught me. I go into the alpha state, where my brain waves slow down and I am in a state of peace and tranquility, which allows me to relax. It works every time. All I have to do is close my eyes, look upwards with my eyes closed. I focus on the spot between my eyebrows. When I feel a slight pressure, I slowly start to count down from 10 to one. When I get to one I am in the alpha state.

~TRAVEL DOWN YOUR PATH~ If you're walking down a path in life and you suddenly realize that you're on the wrong path, retrace your steps and start over on the right path – the path you were meant to take. DO NOT continue down the path and try to make it work for you. You're not a failure if you retrace your steps. On the contrary! It simply means that you're course correcting based on new information.

~READ TO EXPAND YOUR MIND~ I have always enjoyed reading and I move through phases where I focus on a certain topic. About four years ago I came across some information that suggested that we should read a book a week. I have followed and surpassed that guide. I also made the commitment to read broadly. Because of this commitment, I have read books that I found very difficult to read. For example, it took three attempts to read *The Autobiography of Benjamin Franklin* and four attempts to read *Flow: The Psychology of Optimal Experience* by Mihaly Csikszentmihalyi. In both instances, I was glad that I slogged through them because I became a little bit more enlightened.

~INVEST IN YOURSELF!~ Take full responsibility for your professional and personal development. Each year, it's important to take a course, seminar or workshop, not only in your area of expertise, but just for the fun of it. Doing this expands your mind and allows you to think differently. During the past four years, besides courses to help me provide better service to my clients, I have taken an Improv class, a workshop on clowning and another on laughter yoga. These classes have broadened my perspective on life.

~IMPROVE HOW YOU DO THINGS~ About three times a week, spend about 30 minutes brainstorming by yourself to find ways to do your work better. This exercise stretches you, and you'll be amazed by the number of great ideas you come up with.

~TAKE CONTROL OF YOUR MIND~ Something that I stumbled on is that I controlled my mind and it didn't control me. Make the most of your mind and let it work for you. The Zen saying, "Be master of mind rather than mastered by mind" supports my belief. Develop your memory. Develop your potential, work on logic problems and crossword puzzles. You will make yourself more valuable. Learn how to focus.

~LISTEN TO YOUR BODY AND TAKE CARE OF IT~ Listen carefully to your body because it will tell you things. It warns you when you are ill. It tells you when you can go further than you first thought. It serves you well when you serve it well. When was the last time you thanked your feet for taking you where you needed to go?

~SEARCH FOR THE ANSWERS WITHIN~ The first time I heard the saying that the answer lies within, I was frustrated because I didn't know how to access it. Meditation has worked wonders in connecting me to my deeper self. It only works when I am completely relaxed and not worrying about life's stressors. I had a very hard time meditating properly until I learned about guided meditation. After using guided meditations for about three months, I became disciplined and understood how to meditate unguided. As I learned new meditation techniques, I came up with my own version. Once you become comfortable with the practice you'll be amazed how peaceful you feel. Meditation combined with the brainstorming technique allows you to uncover creative solutions to any problem.

~THE IMPORTANCE OF FORGIVENESS~ Forgiveness is the key to becoming fully human, living a fully engaged life, instead of one of mere existence and quiet desperation. When I decided to forgive myself and let the guilt of not being there when my father died melt away, I suddenly felt liberated and lighter. For years, I held the guilt so close to my chest that it became a part of me. When I finally let go of the guilt and forgave myself, I was able to forgive him for not being there, even when he was physically there. This was very cathartic, because I was now able to forgive others. We are not our mistakes; we are simply people who have made mistakes. Forgiveness unbinds you, lightens your load and ultimately frees you. According to William Arthur Ward, a former American college administrator, "Forgiveness is a funny thing. It warms the heart and cools the sting."

~THE IMPORTANCE OF GRATITUDE~ I was amazed at how willing people were when I asked them to allow me to interview them for this book. It made me realize how much I have to be grateful for. Things may not be perfect in our lives, but there is always something for us to be grateful for – it could be a child's smile, beautiful flowers, our health, or a kind word. There's always hope in the midst of despair. Let's focus on the good!

I have attempted to distil the interviews, along with the 12 Avil Beckford Basics into an Itness Funnel as a means of summarizing them.

175

PULLING IT ALL TOGETHER | TABLE 4: ITNESS FUNNEL

13 ITNESS POINTS

1. Listens & Hears
2. Focuses on the task at hand
3. Commits and follow through
4. Cultivates relationships, surrounds himself/herself with the "right" people
5. Understands that there is a higher purpose, and life isn't just about me
6. Takes a holistic approach to life

7. Learns continuously & Reads voraciously
8. Thinks deeply and differently
9. Adapts to different situations
10. Refuses to be satisfied with the status quo

11. Loves and enjoys work and life
12. Knows himself/herself
13. Recognizes vulnerabilities

12 AVIL BECKFORD BASICS

1. Listen & Hear
2. Take a time out
3. Take control of your mind
4. Search for the answers within
5. Tell people you value & appreciate them
6. Listen to your body and take care of it

7. Read to expand your mind
8. Invest in yourself
9. Improve how you do things
10. Travel down your path

11. Practice forgiveness
12. Live gratefully

3 MAJOR THEMES

Focus   Learning   Passion

WHAT YOU ATTRACT
SUCCESS

CELEBRATING YOUR OWN ITNESS

You have read the stories and gotten to know the interviewees a little better, how much of "it" do you have? How many of the 13 ItnessPoints can you integrate into your life? How many of the 12 Avil Beckford Basics do you practice on a regular basis? What kind of life could you lead if you integrated focus, passion and continuous learning into your life?

Set aside an hour and answer the same questions that the interviewees answered.

1. Describe a challenge (business) that you had and how you resolved it.

_____

_____

_____

_____

_____

_____

2. What lessons did you learn in the process?

_____

_____

_____

_____

_____

_____

3. How do you integrate your personal and professional life?

4. In your opinion, what is the formula for success?

5. Describe a major regret that you've had.

6. What's your favourite quote and why?

_____

_____

_____

_____

_____

_____

_____

7. Which book did you read that made a major difference in your life?

_____

_____

_____

_____

179

_____

_____

_____

_____

8. Do you notice any similarities with any of the other interviewees?

_____

_____

_____

_____

_____

_____

_____

9. If you are honest with yourself, where do you fall along the Itness Continuum?

THE ITNESS CONTINUUM

"NON-ITNESS"   "ULTIMATE ENLIGHTENMENT"

SELF EVALUATION

After each set of interviews I have asked you to answer the questions in the Itness Door, did you take the time to do so? The reason that I have done this is to help you raise your level of awareness, as well as make connections to your own life in a very tangible way. By engaging in these activities, I hope that you will recognize opportunities for positive changes in your life.

The stories are a gift to us. They provide insights. They provide wisdom. They provide key learnings that we can apply to our lives.

KEY APPLICATIONS: GUIDELINES TO LIVE BY

- START LIVING TODAY
- Live each day as if it were your last
- Regularly think about what's important to you
- Develop a set of values that you can apply to all facets of your life
- There is never a perfect time to take action, so start now. There is never a perfect situation, so start where you are
- Take time to exercise and enjoy what's around you
- Surprise those close to your heart and do the unexpected
- Schedule time for family and friends
- Establish and nurture relationships with people
- Don't be a workaholic, schedule time for play
- Are your strengths aligned with your interests? Hire a coach if you have to, to help you work through this
- Always try to strike a balance between information gathering and decision-making. Listen, mull over what you've heard, then make your decision
- With each client transaction, ask yourself, "How do I feel about this?"
- Think carefully before you decide to sever a relationship
- Guide your children, but allow them to decide on their vocation in life
- Take time for regular reflection and introspection to learn from your experiences

What are your key applications?

A FTER WORD

Is there original thought? According to Goethe, "Everything has been thought of before, but the problem is to think of it again."

I am always concerned about providing value to others. I always strive to provide the kind of information that will increase people's knowledge. When I was close to completing this book there were some strange coincidences.

Every day I meditate twice for at least 15 minutes, immediately after I awaken and just before I go to sleep at night. During and immediately after meditation, a stream of ideas and insights would flow to me. I got ideas about things to include in this book and how to say it. Some of them were important ideas and insights that I had had previously, but parked because their time hadn't come.

During one meditation, I remembered the visit I had with my friend Julia Watt, where I noticed how she really listened and heard what I had to say. I decided to include that in the section "Things I Know." Immediately after my meditation, I wrote that section mentioning *The Miracle of Mindfulness*. About 30 minutes later I received an email that mentioned Thich Nhat Hanh's *The Miracle of Mindfulness*.

In another example, an ezine that I subscribe to talked about Dr. Masaru Emoto's study on how thoughts affect water, a study mentioned by Lydia Danner in her answer to favourite quote.

I mentioned previously that I found it very difficult to read *Flow: The Psychology of Optimal Experience* by Mihaly Csikszentmihalyi. It took me four attempts in five years to read this book. While I was writing this book, I had an instinct that I should read it. Knowing that I was unsuccessful in three previous attempts, I decided to start at Chapter

Two since I had never gotten beyond Chapter One. I also decided that I would read an entire chapter in one sitting. In the final chapter, the author mentioned that he used Dante's *Divine Comedia* to introduce a workshop he was teaching on midlife crisis. As he described Dante's *Divine Comedia*, it was déjà vu, I could hear Ann Kirkland telling me about the book which influenced her.

I will end this book, the same way that I started. It never occurred to me to write a business book until a colleague planted a seed. It was somewhat of a daunting task to write this book, but I started and here it is. I hope that you like it.

"Reflect upon your blessings, of which every man has plenty, not on your past misfortunes, of which all men have some."

~Charles Dickens

183

APPENDIX A: BOOKS THAT INFLUENCE PEOPLE WHO GET IT

CATEGORY		TITLE	AUTHOR
BUSINESS			
	Organizational Behaviour	*Beyond Certainty: The Changing Worlds of Organizations*	Charles Handy
	Finance	*The Entrepreneurial Journey In Jamaica: When Policies Derail*	Paul L. Chen-Young
	Management/ Leadership	*Winning With People*	John C. Maxwell
	Management	*Your Roadmap for Success*	John C. Maxwell
SELF-HELP/ WELL-BEING			
	Self-help General	*How to Win Friends and Influence People*	Dale Carnegie
	Self-help General	*Key To Yourself*	Venice Bloodworth
	Self-help General	*Power vs. Force: The Hidden Determinants of Human Behavior*	David Hawkins
	Self-help General	*The Magic of Thinking Big*	David J. Schwartz
	Self-help General	*The New Psycho-Cybernetics*	Maxwell Maltz
	Self-help General	*The Power of Positive Thinking*	Norman Vincent Peale
	Self-help General	*The Seven Habits of Highly Effective People*	Stephen Covey
BIOGRAPHY/ MEMOIRS			
	Autobiography	*Still Me*	Christopher Reeve
	Autobiography	*All God's Children Need Traveling Shoes*	Maya Angelou
	Autobiography	*I Know Why the Caged Bird Sings*	Maya Angelou

184

Biography	*Alexander Hamilton: The Year That Rocked The World*	Ron Chernow
RELIGION/ SPIRITUALITY		
Hinduism	*Autobiography of a Yogi*	Paramhansa Yogananda
Zen Buddhism	*That Which You Are Seeking Is Causing You to Seek*	Cheri Huber
Bible Studies	*The Holy Bible*	
Bible Stories	*The Little Soul and the Sun*	Neale Donald Walsh
Bible Studies	*The New Testament*	
Other East Religions	*The Prophet*	Kahlil Gibran
General Religion	*The Way to Love*	Anthony de Mello
COMMUNITY/ CULTURAL STUDIES		
Women's Studies	*Outrageous Acts and Everyday Rebellions*	Gloria Steinem
African-American Studies	*The Destruction of Black Civilization Great Issues of a Race from 4500 B.C to 2000 A.D.*	Chancellor Williams
Women's Studies	*The Female Eunuch*	Germaine Greer
Social Studies	*The Gift: The Form and Reason for Exchange in Archaic Societies*	Marcel Mauss
Women's Studies	*The Women's Room*	Marilyn French
FAMILY/ RELATIONSHIPS		
Family	*The Successful Family: Everything You Need to Know to Build a Stronger Family*	Creflo A Dollar and Taffi L. Dollar
HISTORY		

185

	History General	*The Penguin History of the World*	J. M. Roberts
TRAVEL			
	Travel Literature	*South from Granada*	Gerald Brenan
FICTION			
	Literature - Poetry	*Divine Comedy*	Dante Alighieri
	Science Fantasy	*Lord of the Rings*	J. R. R. Tolkien
	General	*Slaughterhouse-Five*	Kurt Vonnegut
	Literature - General	*The Celestine Prophecy*	James Redfield
	Literature - General	*The Grapes of Wrath*	John Steinbeck

APPENDIX B: BOOK SUMMARIES & PERSONAL REFLECTIONS

INTERVIEWEE: Ann Kirkland

NAME OF BOOK: *Divine Comedy*, Dante Alighieri

Written in the 1300s, it is a very complex book that can be read on many different levels, and it helps to have other people to discuss it with. The man starts out being on a path, which he gets off - he gets lost in the woods. He sees a hill with the sun up there and thinks he can climb up the hill and everything will be fine. But, as he is climbing up the hill he encounters three beasts, a lion, leopard and wolf that chases him back down the hill, and he realizes that he has to go back down through the inferno and up through purgatory until he reaches paradise. *Divine Comedy* is written on a beautiful poetic level, a metaphoric level, a spiritual level, a political level and I love it because the man takes it seriously. He is introspective, he's looking out at the world, he is trying to figure out who he is and he realizes that the world isn't all about just me, me, me, and I want, I want, but there is an obligation attached to it that brings joy. He takes seriously his yearnings for God, for a deeply religious life, but he doesn't take as given, everything that has been handed down to him. He's a huge questioner. To me, *Divine Comedy* is an incredibly inspiring book to give place and room in my life for longings that I've had, but pushed away, but now, I have given much more prominence in my life.

187

INTERVIEWEE: Anthea Rossouw

NAME OF BOOK: *I Know Why the Caged Bird Sings*, Maya Angelou
All God's Children Need Traveling Shoes, Maya Angelou

These two books are a part of a five-volume autobiography. In *I Know Why the Caged Bird Sings*, the central message for my situation is, that if women are caged in by poverty and all the terrible social evils in their community, do they shrivel up and die because of these given circumstances? Or, do they use their hospitality and their humanity and their skills to welcome, to reach out and to be heard outside? And in so doing create their own destiny and a better life.

All God's Children Need Traveling Shoes, Maya Angelou

Only when people travel to South Africa and see how they can reach out via their travels, can we make a difference. We need to take the Kamammas (community matriarchs), and help them to don their travelling shoes, so that they can tell their stories.

INTERVIEWEE: Avil Beckford

NAME OF BOOK: *Key to Yourself*, Venice Bloodworth
The Magic of Thinking Big, Dr. David Schwartz
The New Psycho-Cybernetics, Dr. Maxwell Maltz

Key To Yourself helped me to reconnect with my authentic self. I read this book when I was going through a turbulent period in my life. This book not only gave me hope, but it also taught me how to go "into the silence" to find the answers that I sought.

The New Psycho-Cybernetics by Dr. Maxwell Maltz and *The Magic of Thinking Big* by Dr. David J. Schwartz helped me to cement that re-connection. These three books showed me how to focus on what I am thinking throughout the day. So, instead of focusing on what I do not want in my life these books taught me how to focus more on the things that I do want.

INTERVIEWEE: John Gardner

NAME OF BOOK: *South From Granada*, Gerald Brenan

If I had to choose one book, it would be *South From Granada*. It is not so much what is in the book, but why I remember it. I met my wife in the south of Spain, a country and culture I knew little about at the time. We did not share a common language, but South from Granada dealt with life in a region near where she lived and reading it gave me important insights. The book kept me going, encouraging me to learn Spanish and go back to Spain. Eventually my wife and I were married. Forty years later we are still married, live here in Canada, and have three children and five grandchildren.

INTERVIEWEE: Andrea Nierenberg

NAME OF BOOK: *How to Win Friends & Influence People*, Dale Carnegie

For the past 15 years, I have been reading this book once a year and each time I get something new from it. The book is based on common sense and communication. Essentially, the book tells you how to be more mindful.

INTERVIEWEE: Donald Williams

NAME OF BOOK: *The Entrepreneurial Journey in Jamaica*, Paul Chen-Young

I was an employee of a large Multinational Commercial Bank [Canadian in origin] that had operated in Jamaica for almost 100 years. I had significant exposure and training on good corporate governance, and, at the time when the financial debacle was unfolding, I questioned my exposure and training given to me over the years, as also the BANK'S focus. The book had a very positive impact on me because it confirmed that my training and exposure over the years were correct, and that good financial management would always redound to one's benefit, whether or not it is practised personally, by a corporation or by our government.

INTERVIEWEE: Purdy Crawford

NAME OF BOOK: *Alexander Hamilton: The Year That Rocked The World,* Ron Chernow

This is a biography of an incredible person whom I admire very much. At the age of 13, Alexander Hamilton ran a trading company in the Virgin Islands on behalf of a New York Trading firm, and at 14 he immigrated to the United States. Former Secretary of the Treasury, Hamilton fought in the Revolutionary War with George Washington, created the first financial structure for the United States, and understood the financial structures of the United Kingdom and France. The biography showcases Hamilton's varied life, as well as painting a rich picture of the America that was emerging from the Revolutionary War.

INTERVIEWEE: Asha McLeod

NAME OF BOOK: *The Seven Habits of Highly Effective People,* Stephen Covey

This book is my bible. Because of my negative view of life, I realize that I can always be better. I strive to make myself better. I had to find habits to make me more successful. It teaches me how to interact with my team at work, and shows me how to be a better team player and motivate my apprentices. They work with me and not for me.

INTERVIEWEE: Peter Bouffard

NAME OF BOOK: *The Way to Love,* Anthony de Mello

It's in the context of finding love, it's done within an area that makes it real, and he focuses on love at the point of reality, both in yourself and the other person, rather than aspects of pure romantic desire type love, needy love, and all that other kind of stuff that gets romanticized so much. In the book, you see that love is really about what it gives, what it's like given to you and to the other person.

INTERVIEWEE: Janice Lawrence-Clarke

NAME OF BOOK: *The Successful Family: Everything You Need To Know To Build A Successful Family,* Dr. Creflo A. Dollar and Taffi L. Dollar

This book, together with *The Holy Bible,* has opened my eyes and showed me how to live as a true Christian woman, as well as how to raise my child. It outlines practical ways to live a happy, healthy and prosperous life while building great relationships. It has had, and continues to have a great impact on my life.

INTERVIEWEE: Jim Rohn

NAME OF BOOK: *The Holy Bible*

It's the one book that has had the biggest impact on me. It is filled with history, poetry and excellent love stories. It gives key advice to follow.

191

INTERVIEWEE: Chris Widener

NAME OF BOOK: *The Holy Bible*

It has the stories of the greatest triumphs and the greatest tragedies. It shows the human condition and the human potential. It introduces us to a man - Jesus - whose life and teachings have transformed the world and countless lives. It teaches faith, hope and love. Its teachings have driven the expansion of western culture, the building of countless millions of hospitals, schools, and orphanages to name just a few of the ways that The Holy Bible and its teachings have changed our world. Most importantly for me, when I was a wandering young man, drifting aimlessly but in the wrong direction, it corrected my path and pointed me in the direction I continue in today. It taught me how to handle myself, my relationships, money, work, my family and my mind. It taught me how to live for others rather than for myself. It taught me how to find peace, no matter what storms may face me.

INTERVIEWEE: Claire Hoy

NAME OF BOOK: *The New Testament (The Holy Bible)*

It has been my moral compass and when I have had serious problems I learned from it. It shaped the way that I try to conduct my life. Whenever I have heavy personal issues I reach for it. My moral values are based on *the New Testament.* There are life lessons in the context of teaching you something. It is filled with people facing all kinds of adversities and how to deal with them.

INTERVIEWEE: Gloria Lattanzio

NAME OF BOOK: *The Women's Room,* Marilyn French
The Female Eunuch, Germaine Greer
Outrageous Acts And Everyday Rebellions,
Gloria Steinem

192

These books all dealt with the issue of feminism, and gave me an intellectual framework to understand the role of women in society, and then from there, to begin to socially advocate for an increasing role for women in society.

INTERVIEWEE: Stephen Abram

NAME OF BOOK: *The Gift: The Form and Reason for Exchange in
Archaic Societies,* Marcel Mauss

It talks about the role of gift giving in society and how stories are gifts. You help people through gifts, and the library's role is gifting to the community or to the learner.

INTERVIEWEE: Lea Chambers

NAME OF BOOK: *The Prophet*, Kahlil Gibran

It is a series of poems containing wisdom about all aspects of life and the challenges we face as we go "home." I read it when I was 17 years old and it has always served as a source of inspiration and wisdom, especially in times (and years) when life was really challenging.

INTERVIEWEE: Lea Chambers

NAME OF BOOK: *The Prophet*, Kahlil Gibran

It is a series of poems containing wisdom about all aspects of life and the challenges we face as we go "home." I read it when I was 17 years old and it has always served as a source of inspiration and wisdom, especially in times (and years) when life was really challenging.

INTERVIEWEE: Oliver Campbell

NAME OF BOOK: *The Prophet*, Kahlil Gibran

It was particularly influential in my decision to leave Jamaica and complete my professional exams in the United Kingdom. The author was a very spiritual person who was also blessed with genius. I define genius as someone who has the ability to make complex things simple. Genius resides not only in persons of great intellect, but also in persons with outstanding physical and athletic ability. The genius of Gibran is shown in the simplicity of his writings, which at the same time set out the most profound observations about the human condition.

INTERVIEWEE: Joe Martin

NAME OF BOOK: *Beyond Certainty: The Changing Worlds of Organizations,* Charles Handy

Charles Handy explains that when you get to your mid 50s you shouldn't have a job, but a "portfolio life," which is a portfolio of things to do. Examples of Handy's "portfolio life" include the following:

1. Paid work: remunerated on a time basis
2. Contract work: remunerated according to the results obtained
3. Household work: carried out as part of managing and maintaining a household
4. Volunteer work: done for charity organizations, one's community, friends, family and neighbours
5. Educational work: carried out for purposes of learning, professional development, reading, increasing our level of culture

I decided to take early retirement from being a partner at the consulting firm where I had worked for years. I took Handy's advice and created my portfolio of things to do.

194

INTERVIEWEE: Samy Chong

NAME OF BOOK: *Power vs. Force,* David Hawkins
The Celestine Prophecy, James Redfield

Power vs. Force maps out the skill of consciousness journey of where each of us are, and directs us to what the next step will lead us to. The book calibrates how we continue to live and grow as a human being. It's the most powerful book that I have ever come across in my life.

The Celestine Prophecy started me on this journey and allowed me to really open my eyes to what this journey on earth is really about.

INTERVIEWEE: George Fraser

NAME OF BOOK: *Winning With People,* John C. Maxwell
The Destruction of Black Civilization: Great Issues of a Race from 4500 B.C. to 2000 A.D., Chancellor Williams

Winning With People is about building relationships and is a seminal text to the work that I do – everything is about relationships. Destruction of Black Civilization helped me to understand what happened in Africa, what happened to what was once a great continent.

INTERVIEWEE: Prudence Brown

NAME OF BOOK: *The Power of Positive Thinking,* Norman Vincent Peale
Your Roadmap for Success, John C. Maxwell

The Power of Positive Thinking talks about the need to put the past behind, focus, treat people right, take time out for oneself, pursue your goals relentlessly and include God in everything you do.

Your Roadmap for Success emphasizes that success is not wealth, power or happiness, and not something one acquires, or achieves, but a journey that you take your whole life. Success is knowing one's purpose in life, how to grow to one's maximum potential and sow seeds that benefit others. The recipe in this book has been the yardstick for measuring the success of my life over the years. The book taught me to live one day at a time and live each day as it were the last.

INTERVIEWEE: Heather Resnick

NAME OF BOOK: *Still Me,* Christopher Reeve

I read this book about a year after I had cancer for the second time. The book talks about Christopher's hope. Reading in between the lines I got the bigger picture of understanding what makes people have hope.

INTERVIEWEE: Simon Grant

NAME OF BOOK: *The Penguin History of the World*, J. M. Roberts

It describes the development of civilization and the human race and covers an enormous breadth of material and most of the major events in history.

This book helped me put many things in perspective – how temporary things really are and how much has gone before. We tend to believe that our time is special but there is a cyclic nature to power of nations and ideas and even trends. Much of what we see in the world today has happened before many times before but with different players and environments. We are not as special as we think.

INTERVIEWEE: Seaton McLean

196

NAME OF BOOK: *The Lord of the Rings*, J. R. R. Tolkien
Slaughterhouse-Five, Kurt Vonnegut

The books, which impacted me, include Slaughterhouse-Five by Kurt Vonnegut, and books by Ray Bradbury. In addition, a seminal moment for me was when I read Lord of the Rings as a teenager.

INTERVIEWEE: Gabriel Draven

NAME OF BOOK: *The Grapes of Wrath*, John Steinbeck

Not only is it a beautifully, profoundly written book, but it is also a book about social justice. It's a book about people, about the "haves" and the "have nots", and I have been an underdog all my life.

The story takes place during the depression of the 1930s and it's about a family of subsistence farmers or sharecroppers in Oklahoma. Their son gets out of prison for murdering a guy, and they feel that they are going to lose the farm, be kicked off the farm by the corporation that owns it. They get a handbill, which said that they were looking for help in California, so they decide to all go to California because of the jobs there.

They leave their farm and travel to California to look for work. What they didn't realize was that there were cars traveling across the desert into California like ants. The problem was that everyone was getting the same handbill. As the book unfolds page after page, you sit there and think that no good can come from this, and you turn the page and you think again, no good can come from this. And, the family gets further and further into pure shit, and Steinbeck's brilliance as a writer, is that even though you think that no good can come from this, you are left with the feeling that the family can somehow survive because that's the kind of people they are, and because of the kind of people they come from. It's kind of written into the DNA code of people who survive. It's a brilliant, brilliant book. It's pure genius.

197

INTERVIEWEE: Maria Nemeth

NAME OF BOOK: *Autobiography of a Yogi*, Paramahansa Yogananda

This book is not only about Yogananda's life, but also about the lives of all the spiritually developed people that he met in India and Europe. The book is also about his philosophy, which combines the teachings of the Bhagavad-Gita with Christianity. It was his personal mission to bring what he calls the best of the west and the east together. It's a book that had a profound influence on a number of people's lives. For me, it was a book of such hope and sweetness. No matter what your religious orientation it spoke to the fact that we are all children of spirit, and the best thing for us to do is wake up and see this in our self and in others.

INTERVIEWEE: Lydia Danner

NAME OF BOOK: *The Little Soul and the Sun*, Neale Donald Walsh

There is a saying: "When the student is ready the teacher will appear." Being a fringe dweller, my teachers have always come in the form of books. Probably my favourite is: *The Little Soul and the Sun* by Neale Donald Walsh. It is a children's book, but I believe its message is ageless. I love it so much I always tell the story to others. I also recount it to all of the students in the classes that I teach.

It's a delightful story about a little perfect soul who wants God to grant him the experience of 'forgiveness'. God's explanation of what that would be like is really an explanation of what life is all about and why we are really here. It has had a profound influence on my life because its message resonates with my core spirit. It is in God's words. "I have sent you nothing but Angels".

INTERVIEWEE: **Gail Blanke**

NAME OF BOOK: The Play, *Our Town*

Set at the turn of the 20th century, in the small town of Grover's Corners, New Hampshire, U.S.A., the play reveals the ordinary lives of the people, the tale of love, marriage and death and daily life. The play is centered on a woman, Emily, who dies during childbirth and wants to go back. Those who died before her allow her to go back for a day. Emily chooses to go back on her twelfth birthday. On her twelfth birthday she sees her family and suddenly realizes how much she took things for granted. She didn't appreciate how wonderful she had it at the time. Emily realizes how precious life is.

This play is about seizing the moment and living life fully in the moment. At 10 years old I made the promise, which I have kept, to let those near and dear to me know how much I love and appreciate them.

199

APPENDIX C:
BOOKS WRITTEN BY INTERVIEWEES

Gail Blanke, Lifedesigns, LLC

Between Trapezes

In My Wildest Dreams

Taking Control of Your Life

George Fraser, Frasernet

Success Runs In Our Race: The Complete Guide to Effective Networking in the African American Community

Race For Success; The Ten Best Business Opportunities for Blacks In America

Claire Hoy

A Rebirth For Christianity (Co-authored with Alvin B. Kuhn)

Canadians In The Civil War

Nice Work: The Continuing Scandal of Canada's Senate

Stockwell Day: His Life and Politics

The Truth About Breast Cancer

Clyde Wells: A Political Biography

By Way of Deception (Was Number 1 on New York Times Bestseller's List and Co-authored with Victor Ostrovsky)

Margin of Error: Pollsters and the Manipulation of Canadian Politics

Friends in High Places: Politics and Patronage in the Mulroney Government

Bill Davis, A Biography

Maria Nemeth, Academy for Coaching Excellence

The Energy of Money

Andrea Nierenberg, The Nierenberg Group

NonStop Networking: How To Improve Your Life, Luck and Career

MillionDollar Networking: The Sure Way to Find, Grow and Keep Your Business

Heather Resnick, HRighter Rights the Wrong and Writes the Right

Women Reworked Empowering Women in Employment Transition

Jim Rohn, Jim Rohn International

Twelve Pillars (Co-authored with Chris Widener)
The Five Major Pieces of the Life Puzzle
Leading an Inspired Life
Seven Strategies for Wealth & Happiness
The Seasons of Life
Treasury of Quotes (hardback and excerpt versions)

Chris Widener, Made for Success

The Image
The Angel Inside
Twelve Pillars (Co-authored with Jim Rohn)
Made for Success
Four Seasons
Success Quotes
Live the Life You Have Always Dreamed Of

201

SPECIALIZED BOOKS

Mary Ellen Bates, Bates Information Service

Building and Running a Successful Research Business:
  A Guide For the Independent Information Professional
Super Searchers Cover the World: the online secrets
  of international business researchers
Mining For Gold on the Internet: how to find investment and
financial information on the Internet
Researching Online For Dummies, 2nd edition (co-author,
  with Reva Basch)
Super Searchers Do Business: the online secrets of top
  business researchers
The Online Deskbook: ONLINE Magazine's essential desk reference

Amelia Kassel, MarketingBase

Super Searchers on Wall Street: Top Investment Professionals Share
Their Online Research Secrets

APPENDIX D:
AVIL'S INTERVIEW

"If you don't like where you are, change what you are."
~Henry Knight Miller

~CHALLENGE~ What do you when you've lost the passion for your work? There were signs that I was no longer enjoying my work, but I ignored them. I still performed a great job when I worked on projects, but I didn't enjoy the experience. I knew that writing would play a key role in what I decided to do for a living. The big challenge for me was that I was known for one thing, but wanted to do another. How do I get credibility for what I now wanted to do?

~RESOLUTION~ Whenever I am faced with a challenge I usually go to books for the answers that I need. Meditation has worked well for me. Answers often come to me when I am silent.

202

In addition, I welcomed different project opportunities to discover what my new passions were. When I learned to let go, opportunities started to appear. I was asked to edit a newsletter and I said yes. I realized that if I wanted to successfully change what I did for a living, I would have to work behind the scenes to get the experience and credibility that I needed. I wasn't known as a writer, and, that's one of the reasons why I publish *Ambeck Edge* each month.

~LESSONS LEARNED~

1. Listen to your inner voice because it is your guide

2. Life isn't a struggle if you're doing what you were meant to do

3. Life is too short to be doing things that you do not enjoy

4. If you're traveling down a path for a long time and you suddenly realize that it's the wrong path for you, don't think twice, just turn around and retrace your steps, then go on the path that's right for you. Don't make the best of the wrong path

5. I didn't always have to be in control

~HOW TO INTEGRATE YOUR PERSONAL AND PROFESSIONAL LIFE~ I have one life to live. I work for myself so my personal and professional life are both integrated. However, I often do not have enough balance, which is something that I am working on. I do not take enough time for leisure.

~FORMULA FOR SUCCESS~ A few years ago I desperately wanted to find out the formula for success. At the start of my quest, I wasn't sure how to define success for myself. I knew what some people thought success was, but I couldn't define success for myself.

I read many books, took courses and went to conferences to identify the formula for success. Many of these courses were very good but they didn't work for me. One day, I suddenly realized that success is very personal. Because something worked for one person doesn't mean that it's going to work for you. We are all different and there are sometimes things that are unique to our circumstances. After taking the time to work on myself, I realized that, for me, success had to encompass finances, relationships, health (physical, spiritual and mental), business/career and personal.

After various experiments, I came up with the following ingredients:

• Organized Planning	• Persistence
• Desire	• Self-confidence
• Focus	• Enthusiasm
• Commitment	• Vision
• Discipline	

I have used these ingredients when working on a longer-term goal, and I discovered that to be successful, I also had to add in course correction.

~MAJOR REGRET~ Regret is such a heavy burden to carry that I decided not to play the game of "I should have." But, one thing that I have thought about more than once was the time when I noticed my estranged father at the bus stop as my bus pulled into the bus depot. I hadn't seen him for about five years and I debated with myself about whether or not I should get off the bus and say hi to him. By the time I decided to get off and go and speak to him, it was too late and the bus pulled away from the stop.

What makes this experience regrettable is, that was the last time that I saw him. I do not feel like my father was ever really there for me, even

203

when he lived with us. I cannot even tell if I loved him because I never knew who he was. I never knew what his likes or dislikes were. And the biggest thing is that while he was alive I didn't get to tell him that I forgave him.

It took some time for me to release myself from this burden and look at the lessons learned. The big lesson is to value and appreciate the people in your life, and find ways to show them. Is it really that important to be right? Should you wait for the other person to take the first step toward reconciliation? What if he/she doesn't?

~**FAVOURITE QUOTE**~ I like "For things to change, we must change" by Jim Rohn and "If you don't like where you are, change what you are" by Henry Knight Miller because they tell me that I always have a choice. I can stay in an unacceptable situation or I can reinvent myself.

~**INFLUENTIAL BOOK**~ *Key To Yourself* by Venice Bloodworth helped me to reconnect with my authentic self. I read this book when I was going through a turbulent period in my life. This book not only gave me hope, but it also taught me how to go "into the silence" to find the answers that I sought.

In addition, *The New Psycho-Cybernetics* by Dr. Maxwell Maltz and *The Magic of Thinking Big* by Dr. David J. Schwartz helped me to cement that re-connection. These three books showed me how to focus on what I am thinking throughout the day. So, instead of focusing on what I do not want in my life these books taught me how to focus more on the things that I do want. I have read *Key to Yourself* nine times and each time I see something new.

"For things to change, we must change" ~Jim Rohn

204

MORE FROM
AVIL BECKFORD

Journey To Getting It

A companion guide to *Tales of People Who Get It, Journey To Getting* It is an in-depth workbook, which offers a series of thought-provoking exercises, suggestions, and recommendations to increase one's personal and professional awareness as part of a journey to self-discovery.

Ambeck Edge

A monthly e-newsletter that covers a wide range of topics, *Ambeck Edge* is the inspiration for *Tales of People Who Get It.*

Coming Soon!

People Who Get It Quotables

People Who Get It Quotables is a collection of favourite quotes mentioned by the interviewees in *Tales of People Who Get It* and things worth quoting in their interviews.

205

Readers Are Leaders

Readers Are Leaders is a course for executives that revisits concepts from older books and use them to solve today's problems.

Visit my website at www.ambeck.com

O N HER KNEES

*In the still of the night, she wonders if one person can
make a difference in a world that's gone haywire,
She realizes that she has an obligation to leave the
world a better place than when she first came.
"Where should I start? What should I do?" she asks,
The voice of reason responds, "Start where you are?
Go within and listen. Act on what you hear. Live in
the moment. Be aware of what's going on around
you. Work on yourself first, and then you'll be better
equipped to serve others."*

*In the still of the night, the perfect time for reflection
and introspection, she evaluates her life and wonders if
she is morphing into the person she was meant to be,
She is pleased with herself because she has
accomplished so much,
The voice of reason steps in, "Are you truly the person
your were meant to be? What happened to all those
hopes and lofty dreams you once had? Is success a great
title and income? Is that all you are about?"
She suddenly realizes that somewhere along the way she
started to conform and that's when she lost her way.
She is humbled and on her knees.*

-Avil M. Beckford

INTERVIEWEE INDEX

207

 **SUBJECT INDEX**